THREE GAMES IN MAY

AND A TWENTY-YEAR ODYSSEY THAT DEFINED SIR ALEX FERGUSON'S MANCHESTER UNITED

Cheers Rob

ROB CARLESS

FOREWORDS BY STEVE BRUCE AND NEIL CUSTIS

First Edition.
First published 2023

Published by:
Morgan Lawrence Publishing Services Limited
Ridge House Annexe
16 Main Ridge West
Boston
Lincolnshire
PE21 6QQ
www.morganlawrence.co.uk
email: info@morganlawrence.co.uk
Company number: 12910264

ISBN: 9781838232993

A CIP catalogue record is available for this book from the British Library.

Photographs are courtesy of: Allstar Picture Library Ltd / Alamy Stock
Photo, PA Images, Newscom, Mark Pain, Trinity Mirror / Mirrorpix, Andy
Synnuck, Chris Morley, Dilardo Parhbga, Mark Foster.

Every effort has been made to trace the copyright. Any oversight will be
rectified in future editions at the earliest opportunity by the publisher.

Typesetting by Mathew Mann
Cover design by LCGrapix
Cover photographs are courtesy of: REUTERS / Alamy Stock Photo,
Allstar Picture Library Ltd, PA Images,
Proofreading by Amy Memory

Printed and bound in Bulgaria
by Pulsio Print.

DEDICATIONS

To David James Carless.
4th April 1947 to 21st March 2022.

My father, friend, and my inspiration for everything I do.
Thanks for everything, Pops—an incredible human being.
X

To those who lost their lives in Munich on 6th February 1958—
and to those who survived and will never be forgotten.

Geoff Bent—Player
Roger Byrne—Player
Eddie Colman—Player
Duncan Edwards—Player
Mark Jones—Player
David Pegg – Player
Tommy Taylor—Player
Liam (Billy) Whelan—Player
Alf Clarke—Journalist
Don Davies—Journalist
George Follows—Journalist
Tom Jackson—Journalist
Archie Ledbrooke—Journalist
Henry Rose—Journalist
Eric Thompson—Journalist
Frank Swift—Journalist
Walter Crickmer—United Club Secretary
Bert Whalley—United Chief Coach
Tom Curry—United Trainer
Captain Kenneth Rayment—Co-Pilot (died 15th March 1958)
Bela Miklos—Travel Agent who arranged the trip
Willie Satinoff —United supporter due to join the board
Tommy Cable—Airline Steward

MESSAGE FROM OUR CHOSEN CHARITY
Prostate Cancer UK

PROSTATE CANCER IS the most common cancer in men, and is sadly still killing one man every 45 minutes in the UK. But it's through the support of the football community and people like Rob, that we can change the game and invest in research into better diagnosis and treatments to improve the lives of men with prostate cancer and their families.

We're incredibly grateful to Rob for his generosity, and wish him - and *Three Games In May* - every success.

Matt Holdstock
Sport Engagement Manager at Prostate Cancer UK

The registered charity details are: Prostate Cancer UK is a registered charity in England and Wales (1005541) and in Scotland (SC039332). Registered company 02653887

Contents

Foreword by Steve Bruce   9

Foreword by Neil Custis   11

Preface - Terrace Talking   13

Prologue - 10 Years Before 1999   26

Chapter One - The Events that Shaped the World in 1998   37

Chapter Two - The Sum of All It's Parts!   44

Chapter Three - Red or Dead - Game 1   62

Chapter Four - Red or Dead - Game 3   66

Chapter Five - Red or Dead - Game 6   70

Chapter Six - A Whole New Ball Ache   73

Chapter Seven - Red or Dead - Game 8   82

Chapter Eight - Red or Dead - Game 9   88

Chapter Nine - Red or Dead - Game 10   91

Chapter Ten - Red or Dead - Game 11   95

Chapter Eleven - The Events that Shaped the World in 1999   99

Chapter Twelve - Red or Dead - Game 36   105

Chapter Thirteen - Red or Dead - Game 53   109

Chapter Fourteen - Red or Dead - Game 55   117

Chapter Fifteen - Red or Dead - Game 61   124

Chapter Sixteen - Red or Dead - Game 62   132

Chapter Seventeen - Red or Dead - Game 63   138

Chapter Eighteen - The 1998-1999 Season Overview   166

Chapter Nineteen - The Following Season: 1999-2000   182

Chapter Twenty - Manchester United into the Millenium   197

Epilogue - 10 Years After 1999   217

Acknowledgements   227

Bibliography   231

FOREWORD BY
Steve Bruce
Manchester United Player 1987–1996.

***

I WAS PLAYING for Norwich City in 1987 and had been informed by the club that the likes of Chelsea and Tottenham were interested in signing me. I was giving it some thought and then I was told Manchester United had an interest. My options soon became easier for me as there was only one club I wanted to play for—and that was United.

I recall that there was a certain amount of haggling being done on both sides, and it was the most stressful time for me during the latter part of the year. I just wanted the deal done. Soon enough, it was, and I was officially announced as a Manchester United player just before the busy Christmas period. We all know the size and stature of the club, but it's not until you become a part of it that you realise just how magnificent it truly is, with the most unique support.

Unfortunately, the results didn't quite go our way at times, and the team that Sir Alex had inherited wasn't good enough. The Boss knew this and, luckily, he was given the time to build it. Once you become part of his team, you have to match his work rate and beliefs. You have to buy into Sir Alex. We all felt the pressure that he was under, and we were desperate to put things right for him as well as ourselves.

The 1990 FA Cup run, and subsequent victory, was the game-changer for us. We dug in and never had a home draw. The turning point for me was the fourth-round win at Hereford on a quagmire of a pitch. Then we went on to win the European Cup Winners' Cup and the League Cup over the next few seasons.

But it was the league that The Boss really wanted—and so did we. We came so close in 1992, and we vowed we would not play second fiddle again.

When I meet people, they always ask me about the two late goals that I scored against Sheffield Wednesday towards the end of the 1992–1993 season. That was the moment we realised that we could very well end up as champions and the momentum was firmly with us. I am proud to have played a major part, but it really was a team effort. The very next game was against Coventry City, and we grabbed a 1–0 victory at Highfield Road through a goal scored by Dennis Irwin. This was equally as important as the goals I had bagged against Wednesday. That was our team spirit.

We came so close to winning all three major domestic trophies in the following season. It was an amazing team and was enhanced by the signings of Roy Keane and Eric Cantona, who was really coming into his own.

What I like about the book that Rob has written is that it's not just about those three games in 1999. It recognises that all great dynasties have a building block. The 1994 team laid the foundation for United's subsequent success, and I am immensely proud that I was part of it and made my contributions. It was all about Sir Alex; his vision, and the fact that he never tampered with the core of the team. A lot of us played together for years, and it was such an incredible time to be a footballer. I just wish that I had been a couple of years younger and could have carried on well after I left the club in 1996.

But there are no regrets. How could there be? I was a Manchester United player, after all.

I hope you enjoy reading this book as much as I enjoyed contributing to it.

Steve Bruce

FOREWORD BY
Neil Custis
Manchester United Correspondent for the Sun 1999–present.

***

I TOOK OVER as the Manchester United Football Correspondent for *The Sun* in the summer of 1999. It was a very exciting time to be writing match reports that focused on the triple champions. There was such a buzz around Old Trafford and at away games, not only in this country but all over the world. Everybody wanted to talk about all things United.

When Rob Carless approached me with the premise of this book, I thought that the 20-year angle with those three games in May 1999 as its centrepiece, along with contributions from the fans, commentators, journalists, and, of course, the players, would be an interesting one. It takes the reader back to a unique and wonderful time – allowing those who were there to relive it once more whilst also showing the younger fan base and players of today what can be achieved.

Neil Custis

PREFACE
Terrace Talking

"It's not where you start; it's where you finish. It's not how you go; it's how you land."
From the Broadway Musical *Seesaw*, circa 1973.
Cy Coleman / Dorothy Fields

***

THIS BOOK HAS been some 22 years in the making and has sat comfortably in the back of my mind during all of that time. I have often spoken about it whilst in the company of friends and family, especially when the conversation turns to football, and we embark on a discussion around the following question: "What is the greatest season ever for any club in England?"

I call it 'Terrace Talking', and my favourite venue to hold it in is within the confines of a lovely public house. Although it's not exclusive, 'Terrace Talking' can take place just about anywhere.

Like a lot of things in life, football is subjective, and I appreciate that it runs the risk of being a bit of a loaded question. I have learned to get my timings right when I ask the question. There are some golden rules that I adhere to. Firstly, never ask the question when a friend or family member's team have just lost, as it can distort the answer. Such an emotional game is football!

I will also ask it when I need to move away from such illustrious company. This is either to a) use the toilet, or b) go to the bar. Basically, anywhere when it affords some time for people to really ponder the question. There are so many answers that folk can give. I'm really looking for the unique angle. This gets my attention more than anything. They talk, and I listen. There are a few responses which I file under 'usual suspects'.

I listen with interest when some talk about Liverpool in the 1970s and 1980s. It's salient.

The first real season that I began my now lifelong love of football was the 1974–1975 campaign. At the time, Manchester United were a Second Division club. Their second-tier membership was to run out after just one season, but this enabled Liverpool to take advantage and, thus, begin their upward trajectory towards winning the vast majority of trophies for the next 15 years. The 1975–1976 season saw United back in the top-flight, and whilst this was great news for the fans who had seen years of neglect, it wasn't a happy sight for them to see Liverpool crowned champions of England yet again. Then, the following season, Liverpool retained the title and were also crowned European champions for the first time. United could seek solace in that they did, in fact, thwart Liverpool from winning the Continental treble by beating them 2–1 in the FA Cup final. Do you want to know just what exactly the Continental treble is? Well, I will come to that shortly.

Then there was the 1983–1984 season. Liverpool were crowned league and European champions, as well as retaining the League Cup (Milk Cup). The first of two treble-winning campaigns that Liverpool would experience. The second coming in the 2000–2001 season when they won the domestic double of the FA Cup and League Cup, whilst also winning the UEFA Cup for the third time in their history. A British record.

1983–1984:
First Division: Winners
FA Cup: Fourth Round
League Cup: Winners
European Cup: Winners

Another notable team put forward is the Nottingham Forest side of 1977–1978. Promoted to the First Division the season before, they swept everyone aside as they became champions of England and won the League Cup to boot. And all this, despite them being expected to be at or around the bottom of the league!

In reality, they had won the league with games to spare, and it was quite apparent that earlier in the campaign, it wasn't a case of *IF* they were going to be champions, but *WHEN*.

The following season saw them finish runners-up to Liverpool but retain the League Cup and also, unbelievably, win the European Cup—a feat that they repeated again in 1980. It was an unforgettable couple of years for Forest under the management team of Brian Clough and Peter Taylor. Two consecutive European Cup final wins against Malmo and Hamburg, both 1–0 victories. One cannot imagine a team like Nottingham Forest in the final ever again, but hey, this was the 70s and 80s!

1977–1978:
First Division: Winners
FA Cup: Quarter Finals
League Cup: Winners

Not to be completely outdone by Liverpool, were their Merseyside rivals, Everton. In 1984–1985, they claimed the First Division title and also won the European Cup Winners' Cup. It would have been a treble-winning season for them too, but Manchester United beat the Toffees in that season's FA Cup final thanks to a solitary goal by Norman Whiteside, who ironically signed for Everton a few years later. United had the dubious honour of being the first team to have a player sent off in the FA Cup Final, when Kevin Moran received his marching orders for a two-footed tackle on Peter Reid.

Manchester United do love spoiling a Merseyside treble!

1984–1985:
First Division: Winners
FA Cup: Runners Up
League Cup: Fourth Round
European Cup Winners Cup: Winners

Manchester City's achievements in the 2018–2019 season also features, most noticeably because they were the first team to win the domestic treble in England. It was raining goals at City's games that year, with the vast majority of them going into the opponent's net, as they became the first club in any of Europe's top leagues to pass the 100–goal mark. What made this achievement even more remarkable was that the landmark was reached in January 2019, halfway through the season, when Danilo scored in a 3–0 win against Huddersfield.

City would then go on to surpass a club-record of 156 goals in a single season (set in the 2013–2014 year) when Leroy Sane scored in a 2–0 win against Manchester United on 24th April 2019. Perhaps their dominance and goalscoring prowess during that year was best personified in the FA Cup final, when they swept Watford aside 6–0 at Wembley.

2018–2019:
Premier League: Winners
FA Cup: Winners
League Cup: Winners
UEFA Champions League: Quarter Finals

Chelsea had a torrid time for most of the 1970s and 1980s, hopping between the two top divisions, but made a comeback in the late 1990s. This was cemented in the 21st Century, especially when José Mourinho took the managerial reins in 2004. It really was a golden time for the Blues, with Chelsea winning their first Premiership title in 2005, followed by another one in 2006. However, the arguments for their greatest ever season are centred around the 2009–2010 season under Carlo Ancelotti. The Italian provided a masterclass in football management, bringing the best out of his players as they registered more than 100 goals in the league, finishing the season with a plus goal difference of 71. They also won the FA Cup for the second year in a row, beating Portsmouth 2–0.

Chelsea's 1970 FA Cup winning song was called 'Blue is the Colour'. It certainly was blue for most of the clubs that faced Chelsea in the 2009–2010 season!

2009–2010:
Premier League: Winners
FA Cup: Winners: Winners
League Cup: Fifth Round
UEFA Champions League: Round of 16

There is always interesting debate around Arsenal when it comes to the greatest football season. After all, they achieved the double-double of both the league and the FA Cup twice— in the 1970–1971 and 1997–1998 seasons. They also won the domestic cup double during the 1992–1993 season when they defeated Sheffield Wednesday in both the FA Cup and League Cup Finals. The 1988–1989 season also gets a mention when they needed to go to Anfield on the very last game of the season and beat Liverpool by two clear goals. Failure to do so would have resulted in Liverpool being crowned champions instead. All the other teams in Division One had completed their games, so this really was all or nothing—the winner taking it all. Arsenal won the game by the margin that they needed, courtesy of an 89th minute goal scored by Michael Thomas. Ironically, Thomas would subsequently go on to play for Liverpool.

It is generally agreed that this was the best ever finish to an English league season, and in particular, the pre-Sky era that began in 1992.

It was not the best ever season for Arsenal, though. That accolade goes to the 2003–2004 campaign, although they only won ONE competition that year! Simply known now as the season of the 'Invincibles', Arsenal did not lose a single game in the Premier League, winning a record 26 games and drawing the other 12. However, they didn't fare so well in the domestic cups, losing to Manchester United in the FA Cup semi-final and to Middleborough in the League Cup semi-final over the two legs. Despite losing both semi-finals, it could still be deemed as going far though in both competitions.

Incidentally, the only other team in England to go unbeaten in the top-flight is Preston North End, who achieved invincible status during the very first season of the Football League, way back in 1888.

2003–2004:
Premier League: Winners
FA Cup: Semi-finals
League Cup: Semi-finals
UEFA Champions League: Quarter Finals

Other notable achievements include Tottenham Hotspur, Preston North End, and Aston Villa, who have all successfully won the domestic double of the League and FA Cup; Tottenham in the 20th Century, Preston and Villa both in the 19th Century.

All of the above achievements deserve scrutiny, recognition, time, and praise—regardless of ones' feelings towards the respective clubs. If you love football, then one admires its outputs—it is that simple. I admire those who make the case as to which team deserves the plaudit for having the greatest season ever, even if it is not the team that they necessarily support. There is no right or wrong answer, either. It is what gives us a balance having differences of opinion.

Manchester United have had many great seasons that could have been put forward.

Several books and television programmes have been made on the subject of United's most successful season in 1998–1999. They have all been insightful and brilliant in their own unique way, and I have thoroughly enjoyed reading and watching them. Whether it be reference, almanacs, month by month comprehensive readings, or even fiction, they have all been excellent, informative, and well-written, and I burned the midnight oil on many occasions.

As I did for this book, it wasn't lost on me that the thoughts I had some 22 years ago had not been explored properly in the way that I envisaged them. This was on two fronts, and they were intertwined.

Manchester United played 63 games during that 1998–1999 season. I am including the Charity Shield as this was an important game, not only between the two biggest teams in England at the time, but also by how it set the scene for the impending season, both physically and mentally. The facts are:

After game 60, United had won precisely:

NOTHING! NADA! ZILCH! NIL! ZIP!

United could have left the gameshow with nothing except for a smile on their faces and a "good day out had by all." But not this Manchester United team. Oh no, they didn't get the memo. They wanted more than just the memories. And so it came to pass that:

After **Game 61** United had become **League champions!**
After **Game 62** United had become **FA Cup winners!**
After **Game 63** United became **European champions!**

United had won **THE** treble.

And this is why the achievement is so very different to all the others that have been mentioned. Not only is it a unique achievement—it has never been done before in this country—but it's also about HOW it was done. Apart from a few games, it was not an easy task for Manchester United to undertake. Just look at how many times they had to come from behind in all the competitions that they won. Arguably, the FA Cup final was more like a stroll in the park for United, but this was sandwiched between two games that went all the way, matches they trailed in.

Even if Newcastle United had put up a better fight in the FA Cup final, and the game had gone to penalties, I still don't think it would have thrown the Red Devils off their winning trajectory. The key word that everyone in the club, its supporters and the press were using at the time was 'momentum.' They had been building it since the turn of the year (1999), and they had become unstoppable. Manchester United's season was one of both guts and, ultimately, glory. They had become THE team to watch on terrestrial, satellite, and cable TV. The viewer could simply not afford to take their eyes away from the screen—not even for a second.

One could sense that something was always about to happen, and in a lot of cases, that is exactly what occurred, especially in the dying minutes of matches that they played in. The FA Cup final may have been an easier game for United than some of the others, but their route to Wembley had challenges in abundance. Liverpool at home in the fourth round and Arsenal in the semi-final replay at Villa Park bear testament to this.

All the other teams' achievements that I have mentioned didn't go into the last three games with so much to win and so much to lose. Yes, Liverpool came very close during the 1976–1977 season, and even if they had beaten United in the FA Cup final to claim the Continental treble, it still wouldn't have been as unique as United's in 1999. Liverpool's last game of the season in the league was at Ashton Gate, the home of Bristol City. Liverpool, who led by an Emlyn Hughes goal, were given a standing ovation by the City players. They had already won the league prior to this final game, but Bristol City defeated the champions 2–1.

As great as they were, it didn't come down to the last three games of the season!

It fascinates me beyond fascination that it has never been done before in English football. It would be remiss of me not to mention some notable teams that have also won trebles. It's also important to define what constitutes a treble as well. A treble is when a club team wins three trophies in a single season. A continental treble is when a club wins the national league competition, the main national cup competition, and the main continental trophy. A domestic treble is when a club wins all three national competitions—usually the league title, the main cup competition, and one secondary cup competition.

So, Manchester United most definitely fall into the former. On the other side of the coin is Manchester City, who became the first English side to win a domestic treble.

Only seven European clubs have achieved the feat of the continental treble since 1967. The first being Celtic in that year. Barcelona and Bayern Munich are the only European clubs to have won this treble twice. The other four consist of: Ajax, PSV Eindhoven, Inter Milan, and, of course, the team that we are covering in this book—Manchester United!

In order to begin to write this book, I decided to speak to the people who were there, to hear about what they experienced; the stories they could tell me about that season. I wanted to feel the emotion and let them tell me about what it was like to experience it first-hand. I had a really interesting time meeting up with people, speaking to them on the phone, on Zoom calls, via social media, and through good old-fashioned email! This is THEIR story—a story that encompasses guts, glory, luck, skill, determination, unbreakable bonds, and mental and physical awareness.

It is not just a football story, either. The way that Manchester United went about their business could be a story about any other sport, both at team and individual level. When you stare at defeat for long periods of time but keep your focus and you know it isn't over till it's over, that is all about mental strength as much as it is physical strength. I would always strongly suggest that to find inspiration and sporting excellence, a coach of any sport should show their teams footage of the last 10 minutes of the 1999 Champions League final; the whole of the Champions League semi-final, second leg, in Turin; the FA Cup fourth round and semi-final replay. The Premier League game at Old Trafford to Leicester City, and the way that United came back to beat Tottenham Hotspur in the final game of the season, are also fine examples of digging deep and never giving in, regardless of whether it is shown to a netball team or to a tennis player—basically, any other sport. The Manchester United way in 1998–1999 serves to remind us that anything is possible, and that defeat can be an imposter after all.

I was really interested in speaking to those people who had attended the three final games of the 1998–1999 season. To have been there when your team won three major trophies—not many people can say they have ever witnessed that. The more that I progressed with the book, I strongly felt that there was so much more to discuss, and when I came up with the Red or Dead chapters, I soon began to realise that I also wanted to look at where United had been 10 years before those remarkable events in May 1999—and where it took them to a decade later. Therefore, the prologue and the epilogue sections look at 1989 and 2009, respectively. This is an important timeline as it allows us to look at the three great teams that Sir Alex Ferguson built. So, in this respect, the quote from the musical *Seesaw* is not entirely accurate. Yes, it depicts those last three games in May and is the centrepiece of the book. However, the story begins 10 years earlier, in December 1989, when 64 balls were put into a bowl with the aim of pairing teams together for 32 matches in the third round of the FA Cup.

Just hearing about the sense of doubt from supporters coming away from Wembley in August 1998, after the mauling against Arsenal in the Charity Shield, it was so palpable that fans were questioning if Alex Ferguson had taken the club as far as he could.

Was the signing of Jaap Stam a bad one?

Would Arsenal now become THE dominant team in England?

I felt that this book needed chapters on at least 10 games of the season that were pivotal in the run-up to those three games in May. I chose the 10 games that were significant in terms of the teams that United faced, the result on that day, and what it actually meant for the season as a whole.

It was a *Sliding Doors* moment—were United Red or were United Dead?

It will come as no surprise to note that this book features a number of games against Arsenal, for they are all significant. It is indeed a game against their North London rivals in which I believe that THE defining moment of the season for Manchester United unfolded.

The ultimate in *Sliding Doors* moments—all of this is captured in Chapter 13, on a night in the West Midlands in April 1999.

On a final note, in this preface, I feel that it is a salient time to home in on just why Manchester United are so revered around the world. They certainly dine at the very top table with a select few peers that include Real Madrid, Bayern Munich, Barcelona, Liverpool, A.C. Milan, and Juventus, to name but a few. Apart from the obvious successes of these teams, there is a common theme when it comes to supporting them. There can be no grey areas—it is very black or white. In his 2021 book, *'Not for me, Clive'*, ITV's main commentator, Clive Tyldesley, makes a very poignant claim: "A club like United splits loyalties due west and east. There are no inhabitants of the middle ground. Nobody "quite likes" United or Liverpool or Bayern. The voting slip for the games Super-Clubs has only two boxes. For or against. The first responsibility of the standard-bearer of such an organisation is to recognise and respect that. The second is to defend their organisation against the rest of the world, even via the indefensible at times. That is all that Sir Alex ever did during his 27 years in charge at Old Trafford. Fiercely, coldly, even mistakenly at times, but always corporately."

It is hard to offer a counterbalance to what Clive Tyldesley wrote in his book. Time and time again, there have been examples of club protection managed expertly by Sir Alex Ferguson and his team around him. Think Eric Cantona at

Selhurst Park in a midweek Premier League game in 1995, or David Beckham at West Ham United in 1998 after the World Cup finals in France. Walls simply did not come tumbling down at Old Trafford under the tenure of Sir Alex. Neither did it happen in training sessions at the Cliff, or near the picturesque village of Carrington, where United moved to in 2000.

Millions around the world love Manchester United. Whether this is out of adversity due to the tragedies that befell the Busby Babes on 6th February 1958, or what occurred during the sixties, with the holy trinity of Law, Best, and Charlton; or could it be Fergie's Fledglings in the mid-1990s? Apparently, you win nothing with kids! Was it the mavericks like Cantona or Ronaldo? In reality, it could be just one of these things—but it could also be all of these things, or it could well be something else. Every United fan I have spoken to has their own reason for their devotion.

Manchester United were relegated from the topflight in the 1973–1974 season, a mere six years after becoming the first English team to win the European Cup. It still seems very strange to even write this down, even after all these years. Images of a less-than-celebratory goal from Dennis Law, wearing the colours of Manchester City, are forever etched in the minds of United fans. Even if it wasn't actually the goal that sealed their fate and relegated them—it's almost an urban legend and the bitterest of pills for the whole club and its supporters to swallow.

However, even if United hadn't renewed their First Division membership (within 12 months), they were still 'A-listers' and remained the team to beat. They finished their solitary season in the second tier in pole position, with Aston Villa and Norwich City taking to the podium in second and third place, respectively. Don't forget, there were no play-offs in those days. As a point of interest, these were the exact same three teams who occupied the top three places (in the same order) in the 1992–1993 season in the inaugural FA Premier League season.

So, whether you love them or hate them, if you are a fan of the beautiful game then you simply MUST respect Manchester United for what they have given, not only to our beautiful game but to the world. This might sound strange, but I have always likened them to Lennon and McCartney. Please bear with me on this one.

You can go to the most far-flung places on earth, and you'll meet someone who will know and be able to sing a Beatles song. And whilst you are roaming these lands, you will find someone wearing a Manchester United replica shirt. I know people that have told me in the past that they have been in Malaysia or Hong Kong, and they have walked the streets surrounded by massive billboards or images on the side of buildings, featuring the likes of Ryan Giggs, Cristiano Ronaldo, or David Beckham. They are not the only club to have worldwide appeal, but I would argue that they have more followers in the world than any other English club.

Television has also played a major part in United's global success; worldwide deals became prominent during the 1990s and 2000s, and with the Red Devils winning a large proportion of the trophies on offer at the time, it's not hard to understand why they became so popular around the world.

In 2013, Kantar, a research company, conducted a worldwide survey, at the request of Manchester United, to investigate just how many fans the club actually has.

The company polled nearly 54,000 adults in 39 countries. The method taken was either face-to-face or online. It then took the figures for each of the countries in the survey and then added in the rest of the world, taking into consideration how popular football was around the globe and if people from those countries actually played for United in some capacity. Very often, a large part of a nation gets behind the team that one of its sons or daughters plays for.

The results were staggering. Based on a population of five billion adults, the company estimated that 659 million of them supported Manchester United! Wow! Kantar reported that half of them (325 million) lived in the Asia-Pacific regions, 173 million in the Middle East and Africa, 90 million in Europe, and 71 million in the Americas. Kantar's director, Richard Brinkman, explained this staggering figure and justified why his company had been tasked with carrying out the survey. "I would back my figures and argue (that they are accurate) to within a 1% margin for error." Brinkman continued, "We work for a number of the largest companies around the world. It's in our interest to produce an accurate figure, not the biggest figure. We need to have more credibility than that."

The publication caused a stir, with many questioning why Kantar had used the word 'follower' and not 'fan' in its survey and arguing that the figures were massively inflated as a result. Brinkman conceded that 'followers' can also follow several clubs. For the purpose of the survey, United's commercial director, Richard Arnold, confirmed that 'followers' were defined as "people who, unprompted, named Manchester United as a team they follow." However, even allowing for a 20% variance, the base is still massive at 527.2 million. One could argue that even half the figure of 659 million is still staggering.

A report published by the Statista Research Department on 31st March 2021, reported on the number of social media followers of the club in November 2019:

Facebook likes: 73.28 million
Instagram Followers: 32.18 million
Twitter Followers: 20.52 million

Whichever research is undertaken, it cannot be denied that millions of people love the club, whether they are 'fans' or 'followers'.

Manchester United is, indeed, definitely a football club of behemoth stature.

PROLOGUE
10 Years Before 1999

"And here's to you, Mrs Robinson."
(Paul Simon)

***

THE THIRD ROUND of the FA Cup is possibly the most exciting of cup draws. It's a meeting point for all the Davids and Goliaths. It is where non-league clubs that have an average attendance of 2,000 are drawn at home against one of the giants, whose average attendance is maybe 50,000. It is where the painting and decorating (his chosen profession in the week) centre-forward can make a name for himself by scoring against the goalkeeper, who does not have to rely on any other income. Your team may go all the way to the final, but it's that third-round draw that excites you, and the one you'll probably remember the most.

If your team is struggling, the draw and the build-up to the game itself help you to forget those woeful performances in the league during the first half of the season. The third-round draw can be most cathartic to those on the terraces—and to those on the pitch.

The third-round draw in December 1989 meant that Alex Ferguson's Manchester United would have to travel to Brian Clough's Nottingham Forest just after the New Year break in January 1990. The two sides had faced each other the season before in the FA Cup quarter-final. United were drawn as the home team, and Forest were vying to reach the semi-final for the second consecutive season. Nottingham Forest kept alive their outside chances of a unique domestic treble by beating the

Red Devils 1–0, with Garry Parker scoring the only goal in the 42nd minute. That defeat ended Manchester United's hopes of silverware for the 1988–1989 campaign, a season in which they had failed to feature in the title race. Shortly after this game, Gordon Strachan, who had been a pivotal part of United's midfield, joined Leeds United.

That failure to mount a title challenge again during the 1989–1990 season was evidence once more that Manchester United were not quite there yet. It was being noticed by not only the fans but also the national media. Just how long would it take for the United board to take a similar note themselves? Just a few weeks after the FA Cup draw had been made, on Boxing Day 1989, United played Aston Villa away. There were no glad tidings for the Red Devils, who were soundly beaten 3–0 by a Villa team who were themselves very much in the title race. "Fergie Must Go" was chanted by the travelling United fans standing in the lower North Stand when the third goal was conceded.

Manchester United were to play two further games in the league before the FA Cup tie at Forest; a 2–2 draw at home to Wimbledon, with Mark Robins scoring the last Manchester United goal of the 1980s, followed by a goalless draw at Queens Park Rangers on the first day of 1990. United started the new decade lying in 15th place of the First Division.

The FA Cup tie between Nottingham Forest and Manchester United, held on 7th January 1990, was chosen by the BBC to be their live game. Forest were clear favourites, and the talk in the studio before the match centred around Alex Ferguson being sacked if his United team failed to progress to the fourth round. The stakes could not have been higher for Ferguson. Jimmy Hill was a pundit that day and remarked that Manchester United didn't look good in the pre-match warm-up. The country sat back knowing that this would probably be Alex Ferguson's last game in charge of the Red Devils if the result did not go his way.

Maybe the comments made by Jimmy Hill had somehow got through to the players on the pitch by the time the match kicked off, because they took the game to Nottingham Forest. Despite United's dominance, the first half remained goalless. As it turned out, there would only be one goal, and that came in the 56th minute when Mark Robins headed the ball home, much to the relief of his manager and the fans in the stadium and watching it all over the world. Manchester United had avenged the previous season's defeat to Forest in the FA Cup. That goal wasn't the best that Ferguson had seen his team score since he took over in November 1986, but it was probably the most important. It was United's first win in nine games, a victory that ensured United progressed to the fourth round. It also meant that the football obituaries that had already been written and ready to print on the back pages of the following day's newspapers would need to be changed—for the time being, at least.

Mark Robins had scored the first Manchester United goal of the 1990s, just as he had grabbed the club's final goal of the previous decade. That certainly is something he will remember for a very long time.

Ferguson had faced his Waterloo and won, but it wasn't enough. He knew that he would have to do this in each of the other rounds as well. His mindset was always to turn United into the number-one club in the league, something that was far from becoming a reality in January 1990. So, his redemption would have to be the FA Cup, and he had to win it at all costs. He had not won a trophy during his four years since taking over at Old Trafford. In fact, Manchester United had not won a trophy since the 1984–1985 season when they beat Everton 1–0 in the FA Cup final under Ron Atkinson. The best chance that they had since then was in the 1987–1988 season when they had finished as runners-up to Liverpool in the First Division, but this was not a close contest, and the final difference was nine points.

The FA Cup was something that they would have to win—for the sake of Alex Ferguson's job and for Manchester United as a club.

The fourth-round draw saw United away once more and a fixture that firmly goes under the 'banana skin' section. This time their opponents were a fourth-division side, Hereford United, whom they faced on 28th January 1990. Another away game and another 1–0 victory, courtesy of an 84th minute winner scored by Clayton Blackmore. Yet again, Ferguson had found himself facing the sack if they failed to win that game, especially having just lost to Norwich City in a televised game 2–0 in the league. United had passed the test again, by a single goal on their travels—but only just.

United would clock up more miles in the fifth round, as this time they would be visiting second-division Newcastle United on 18th February 1990. Again, a single-goal victory was afforded to the Red Devils, but this time it would be 3–2. Mark Robins gave United a 1–0 lead at half-time before the Magpies equalised in the 50th minute through a Mark McGhee penalty. Danny Wallace restored United's lead in the 60th minute. Newcastle came back and levelled the score for a second time just five minutes later through Kevin Scott. The thrilling contest was finally settled in the 77th minute when Brian McClair bagged the winning goal. The chants of "Fergie Out" diminished as the Old Trafford faithful's thoughts began turning to 'is this our year for the cup?'

The quarter-final saw United once more drawn as the away team. This time their opponents would be Sheffield United on 11th March 1990, and it followed the same pattern as rounds three and four, with United winning 1–0 and Brian McClair scoring the winning goal just as he had done in the previous round.

Manchester United dared to dream, and the semi-final would see them paired with Oldham Athletic. The Latics had knocked out high-flying Aston Villa in the quarter-final, and Ferguson remained optimistically cautious as Wembley beckoned. The semi-final was played at Maine Road, of all places, on 8th April 1990, and it proved to be a high-scoring classic, with both teams sharing six goals. Earl Barrett opened the scoring for Oldham in only the fifth minute. United equalised just before the half-hour mark via Bryan Robson. Neil Webb then put United into the lead on 72 minutes, only for Oldham to level through Ian Marshall with just nine minutes remaining on the clock. There would be no further goals, and the game went into extra time. Manchester United made an immediate impact when Danny Wallace made it 3–2 in the opening minutes of extra time before Roger Palmer equalised in the 107th minute. The game was pulsating, and with both teams going for the win, a draw was a fair result. And so, just three days later, both teams would head back to Manchester City's ground to lock horns once more. Brian McClair gave United a lead in the 50th minute, and just like in the first game, Oldham scored on 81 minutes to level the tie, and just like the first game, the match would go into extra time. Mark Robins had set United on the road to Wembley in the third round to effectively save Alex Ferguson's job, and now he would score the winning goal six minutes before the end of extra time to ensure that United actually got there.

Manchester United finished the season in 13th place in Division One but would contest the FA Cup final on 12th May 1990, where they would face Crystal Palace, who were managed by a former United favourite, Steve Coppell. Palace had equally offered up a semi-final spectacular themselves—defeating Liverpool 4–3 at Villa Park in another classic FA Cup match that went into extra time.

The final would find both teams in similar moods to entertain on a boiling hot day in May at Wembley, with both sides serving up a feast of goals. Gary O'Reilly gave the Eagles the lead in the 18th minute before Bryan Robson levelled just after the half-hour mark. Both teams went into the break fairly happy with the first 45 minutes. Mark Hughes put United in front in the 62nd minute before Ian Wright grabbed the equaliser 10 minutes later. No team could force the winner in 90 minutes, and the game went into extra time once more. Ian Wright once again got on the scoresheet, giving Palace the lead just after the restart before Mark Hughes scored his second of the game when he made it 3–3 in the 109th minute.

The replay took place on Thursday 17th May 1990, at Wembley. The major change for the replay was that Ferguson axed his goalkeeper, Jim Leighton, and replaced him with Les Sealey. Ferguson's rationale was that he had noticed that mistakes made by Leighton seemed to hang heavy on the Scottish shot-stopper's mind, and Ferguson didn't want anything to get in the way of United's first real chance of silverware since 1985. After the first game, Ferguson noticed that Leighton was sitting in the Wembley dressing room with his head in his hands. In his 1999 autobiography, Ferguson described Leighton as looking "completely shattered." There had been no reaction when the gaffer had patted his goalkeeper on the back. It bothered Ferguson, and he noticed that Leighton's demure was the same at the after-match reception. The gaffer decided to inform his assistant, Archie Knox, that he was thinking of changing his 'keeper for the cup final replay. Knox tried in vain to talk his boss out of it. However, although Ferguson conceded that Les Sealey was technically not a better goalkeeper than Jim Leighton, he had more confidence, and that was important to Ferguson when it came to cup finals. Ferguson had been a winner when he managed Aberdeen a few years earlier, and he wasn't afraid of making tough decisions that would benefit the team as opposed to appeasing an individual. The great Scotland and Celtic manager, Jock Stein, had once informed Ferguson that he would not entertain the idea of going out and socialising with his team. As long as they performed on the pitch, that was all that mattered to him. Stein was correct, of course. It was not a popular decision, but the result in the replay did, in fact, vindicate Alex Ferguson.

If the first game had been played at a pace similar to those songs that were being played in clubs and raves in Manchester at the time, then the replay was more like the slow section at the local disco. The game was settled in the 59th minute with a goal scored by Lee Martin. Just over half an hour later, referee, Allan Gunn, who had also officiated the first match, blew the final whistle. United had won by a solitary goal, just as they had done three times on the road to the final. This was to be Manchester United's seventh FA Cup victory and their first trophy in five years. Moreover, it was the first trophy won under the guidance of Alex Ferguson. Little did Ferguson know at that precise moment in time just how many more would be added to the trophy cabinet over the coming years. Ferguson had been written off on more than one occasion during that 1989–1990 season, and the team, that according to Jimmy Hill had looked poor in the warm-up of that pivotal day in Nottingham, had defied the odds and won the FA Cup.

Alex Ferguson knew that it would take time to get his team to where he wanted them to be, but for now, he was an FA Cup winner, and that allowed him to look forward rather than over his shoulder. He could plan and really take United to the 'Promised Land' of great success in the new decade.

It would take time, but he had earned the right to continue the journey.

Whilst he sipped the cold victorious bottles of Champagne

with his players on 17th May, he knew that the header from Mark Robins in the 56th minute at Forest was a defining moment and a turning point for him as well as the club. Although, perhaps, he didn't realise just how big that moment would be.

Alex Ferguson was not the only one—but the times were a-changin'!

Although United had come second in the 1987–1988 season, it wasn't really a close contest between them and Liverpool, who won the league by nine points. It was a much closer story in the last season before the start of the Premier League, the 1991–1992 season. The previous campaign had seen Manchester United finish in sixth place, and it was their first top-six place since 1988. They would finish runners-up to Leeds United in 1992, but this time the gap was smaller and the contest fiercer. On 26th April, Leeds beat Sheffield United in a thrilling encounter by 3–2, and they were confirmed as champions when the news came through that Liverpool had beaten United 2–0. Leeds finished on 82 points and Manchester United on 78. The Red Devils were smarting, and once again, the bridesmaid. It would take the emergence of the Premier League to sweep them off their feet in the following season.

Trophies had been won, and youngsters like Lee Sharpe and Ryan Giggs were breaking through and mixing it up with the likes of Bryan Robson, Paul Ince, Mike Phelan, Steve Bruce, Gary Pallister, and Mark Hughes. United had made some exceptional signings in the shape of Peter Schmeichel, Dennis Irwin, Paul Parker, and Andrei Kanchelskis. Experience had been gained, and what didn't kill them made them stronger. Now they were going to set their sights on being the best in this new era of English Football.

At the start of the 1992–1993 season, United splashed out £1 million to secure the services of Dion Dublin from Cambridge United. However, the likeable centre-forward suffered a broken leg very early on in his United career. This unfortunate event made Ferguson active in the transfer market earlier than he would have wished. Eric Cantona had been instrumental in helping Leeds to win the previous season's league title at the expense of Manchester United, and in November 1992, he joined the Red Devils for a reported fee of just £1 million. The Leeds faithful were up in arms and saw this as very much a mistake made by the Leeds United board and their manager, Howard Wilkinson. At the time of the mercurial Frenchman's arrival, United were sitting around the mid-table of the league. However, it was to be a turning point and the missing piece of the jigsaw.

United shot up the league, and it was soon to be a three-horse race involving them, Aston Villa, and Norwich City. Three became two on 5th April 1993, when United effectively knocked Norwich out of the race with an emphatic display at the home of the Canaries, 3–1. Perhaps it would be the very next match that really determined where the championship would go. On Saturday 10th April, both United and Villa were at home; United played Sheffield Wednesday and Villa played Coventry City. Villa did everything but score in the game, hitting the bar and post and camping in the Sky Blues' half. The game ended goalless. United were a goal down as the final whistle blew at Villa Park, courtesy of a penalty converted by John Sheridan. A significant amount of injury time was added due to various stoppages. It was advantage Aston Villa, until up popped Steve Bruce to put himself into United folklore history. John Hilditch had started the match as a linesman but took to the field to take on the role of Referee after Michael Peck was injured on the hour mark. A match ritual for Ferguson's assistance, Brian Kidd was to stop his watch so it would match that of the Referee during the game. He informed his boss that there would be at least six minutes of injury time in the 87th minute. On that occasion, Kidd had not called it correctly, and Hilditch would play significantly more. Then, Steve Bruce scored the equaliser in the 96th and the winner in the 97th minute, although they were officially classed as 86th and 90th-minute goals for some reason. Both were towering headers and sparked jubilant celebrations.

After Steve Bruce had scored his second and winning goal, Old Trafford rejoiced in wild celebrations, none more so than the United manager and his assistants, who punched the air with delight. Kidd's momentum took him onto the pitch, where he fell to his knees with his hands in the air, and weirdly looked like he was on the cover of the hit movie poster of *Platoon* for a brief second or two.

Manchester United went on to lift their first title in the top league after 26 years by a clear 10 points, and in fact, actually won it without kicking a ball when a Nicky Henry goal was enough to give Oldham Athletic a 1–0 victory at Villa Park on 2nd May 1993. The next evening would see a party atmosphere at Old Trafford as United strolled past Blackburn Rovers 3–1. Manchester United were the champions of England in the 1992 –1993 season. A fourth trophy in four seasons under Ferguson had been achieved.

The next season saw Manchester United claim two more trophies, actually making it six in five seasons. And it was very nearly seven! The summer of 1993 was the first of many seasons that were to come in that United would purchase players from a real position of strength—as champions The first player to come through the door was Roy Keane. The Nottingham Forest central midfielder immediately justified his tag as the most expensive footballer in England at the time, as he established a formidable partnership with Paul Ince and was the perfect replacement for Bryan Robson. David May was the other signing.

In the previous season, United hit the top spot on 9th January 1993, after an emphatic 4–1 victory over Tottenham Hotspur at Old Trafford. They would share this with Aston Villa and Norwich City until that win over Sheffield Wednesday, and they didn't concede ground from that moment on. This time, it would take only four games for United to reach the summit after a 2–1 victory over Aston Villa at Villa Park, with Lee Sharpe scoring both goals. They would not go any lower in the league table as they romped to a second consecutive league title, winning it in far greater style, although it was by just eight points as opposed to the previous season's 10, with Blackburn Rovers as runners-up. United's points tally was 92, with 27 wins, 11 draws, and just four defeats. They scored 80 goals and conceded just 38 in the 42 matches, with a goal difference of +42. Not only had United maintained being champions of England, but they also actually improved upon it. In the 1992–1993 season, they had played the same 42 games but had won 24, drawn 12, and lost six times. The points tally was 84, and they had scored 67 whilst conceding 31. The goal difference was +36.

There is a school of thought that suggests that defending a title win is harder than winning it in the first place. United had passed this test with flying colours, and they were to be victorious in the FA Cup as well. Sheffield United, Norwich City, and Wimbledon were all beaten on away soil before United put paid to Charlton Athletic's chances at Old Trafford 3–1 in the sixth round on 12th March 1994. It would be a repeat of the 1990 semi-final when United were paired with Oldham Athletic. The game was played at Wembley on 10th April, and just like the first game, it went into extra-time. The game had finished goalless in the 90 minutes, and it looked like Neil Pointon's goal would be enough to exact revenge for the Latics as the end of extra-time approached. Then, in the 119th minute, Mark Hughes struck the equaliser and the game would go to a replay like it had done four years previously. The replay was held at Maine Road on 13th April. No extra-time was required in this one, as Dennis Irwin and Andrei Kanchelskis put United two goals up after just 15 minutes. As in the first semi-final just three days before, Neil Pointon put himself on the scoresheet five minutes before the break. However, any nerves that may have given United were killed off in the 62nd minute through Bryan Robson, and five minutes later, Ryan Giggs added a fourth to make the final score 4–1.

The final was played on Saturday 14th May 1994, at Wembley, and the opponents were Chelsea. It was at a time when Chelsea were just coming out of their slumber after many years of promotion and relegation, and the final proved to be too soon for them to offer a serious challenge to United. The first half ended goalless, but it was total domination from the Red Devils in the second half. United were awarded two penalties in the 60th and 66th minute, and both were converted by Eric Cantona. Manchester United were in cruise mode just three minutes later when Mark Hughes made it 3–0, before Brian McClair converted in the last few minutes to give United a 4–0 victory on a rain-soaked Wembley pitch. In doing so, United became only the sixth team to do the double after Preston North End, Aston Villa, Tottenham Hotspur, Arsenal, and Liverpool.

They almost won the domestic because, in the League Cup, United saw off challenges from Stoke City, Leicester City, Everton, Portsmouth, and Sheffield Wednesday to reach their second League Cup final in two seasons. The final was contested on 27th March 1994, at Wembley, and it was Aston Villa who stood between them and another trophy. United had pipped Villa to the League title the season before, but it was the team from the Midlands who would come out on top to claim their fourth League Cup. Dalian Atkinson had given Villa the lead on 26 minutes, and they extended this lead on the 76th minute through Atkinson's strike partner, Dean Saunders. United reduced the deficit on the 83rd minute when Mark Hughes scored. However, any ideas of a comeback were well and truly dashed in the closing minutes when Andrei Kanchelskis handled on the line and was duly sent off. Dean Saunders converted the resulting penalty to give Villa victory 3-1.

The building process put together by Alex Ferguson had reaped its rewards and then some. The 1993–1994 season had given United spectacular successes. They would repeat the double again in 1995–1996, (they were League Champions again in 1997) but the class of '94 is held in great esteem and truly can call itself the first great team that Alex Ferguson built. One of the key factors as to why it's not held as highly as the late 1990s and late 2000s teams is that the team didn't do so well in Europe. They had won their first-round match against Hungarian champions, Kispest Honvéd, 5–3 on aggregate, before going out on the away goals rule in the second round. This time they would play the Turkish team, Galatasaray. The first leg ended 3–3 at Old Trafford but a goalless second-leg meant that the Turks progressed instead of United.

In the middle part of the 1990s, United did not have the best of times in European competitions. In the 1994–1995 season, United failed to get out of their qualifying group in the Champions League in the first year that the format had changed to qualifying groups. The following season saw United lose in the first round of the UEFA Cup to the Russian team, Rotor Volgograd. Again, it would be decided on the away goal rule but this time it would be 2–2. United fared much better back in the Champions League in the 1996–1997 season, as they reached the semi-final only to be beaten 2–0 on aggregate by the German team, Borussia Dortmund. In the 1997–1998 season, United reached the quarter-final before once again going out on the away goal rule to the French team, AC Monaco, 1–1 on aggregate. They were getting closer and closer.

CHAPTER ONE
The Events that Shaped the World in 1998

"Curry, cheese and scoring one more than you!"
Fat Les (unofficial England World Cup '98 song)

***

SMOKERS IN CALIFORNIA would have to make the most of being able to do this in certain places in 1998. A new law had been approved that would ban the leisure activity from all bars and restaurants, as well as card houses, from the first day of the following year. Manchester United fans living in California would be forgiven for being a little miffed by wanting to toast the engagement of Victoria Adams and David Beckham in the comfort of their favourite bars whilst puffing on their chosen brand of cigarette.

Staying in the US, the search engine Google was incorporated as a private company. It was perfect timing as the company grew at a rapid pace. It was successful due to a unique algorithm that calculated a website's relevance to a search by analysing links back to the site rather than connections to the search terms, producing higher quality results.

How do I know that? Well, I 'Googled' it, of course!

Major tech news in 1998 also included Microsoft being valued at £261 billion by the New York Stock Exchange, making them the biggest company in the world at the time.

The International Space System (ISS) was launched. This is where NASA sent a six-person crew on the Space Shuttle,

Endeavour, to attach the American Unity node to the Russian Zarya module. The mission, known as STS-88, carried the node up to the Zarya module which had already been launched. The crew completed three spacewalks to connect the first two building blocks of the ISS. The ISS has been continuously manned since 2000. It is not known if they found extraterrestrial life wearing Manchester United replica shirts whilst singing Beatles songs. It would not come as a surprise if they did, though!

1998 witnessed a truly historic event regarding the troubles in Northern Ireland when the Good Friday Peace Agreement was signed by the United Kingdom, Southern Ireland, and Northern Ireland. The Good Friday Agreement, also known as the Belfast Agreement, was signed on 10th April and came into force on 2nd December 1999. The agreement marked the beginning of the peace process between Ireland and Great Britain, as it outlined how the government would work in Northern Ireland. It established that Northern Ireland would have its own Assembly and run a devolved multi-party democratic government with the United Kingdom. The citizens of Ireland and Northern Ireland approved the agreement in referendums held during May 1998.

The European Court of Human Rights (ECHR) was established as a permanent fixture in November 1998. The ECHR was tasked with upholding the observance of basic rights like freedom of speech and the right to a fair trial within the 47 member states of the Council of Europe. It was made permanent in 1998 to help handle the increasing number of cases that were being submitted. The ECHR is also known as the Strasbourg Court as it is located in Strasbourg, France.

Continuing with the European theme, a single currency called the Euro was introduced in 1998, as well as the Central European Bank with its headquarters located in Frankfurt, Germany.

New television shows that made it into our living rooms in 1998 included *Will and Grace, Dawson's Creek,* and *Sex and the City.* All of these shows were extremely popular as they made their way across the pond from the United States. British TV shows that made their debut in 1998 were *The Royale Family* and *Dinner Ladies.*

Cher had the best-selling single of the year with 'Believe' which stayed at number one in the UK for seven weeks. And the Corrs took the honours in album sales with 'Talk on Corners'.

Titanic was THE film of 1998, and other notable Box Office successes were *Deep Impact, Godzilla, Armageddon*, and *Saving Private Ryan*. A special mention must go to Guy Richie when he released his debut film in 1998, *Lock Stock and Two Smoking Barrels*, a cockney crime caper that introduced us to Jason Statham. For some reason, he decided to take a punt on giving one of football's hard men a starring role, and it worked deliciously. Vinnie Jones started his working career as a hod carrier before switching to football, where he played for Wimbledon, Leeds, and Chelsea and also represented Wales at international level. To say that giving the role of 'Big Chris' to Jones, who had no acting experience, was a little left field and a massive gamble, is somewhat of an understatement. But Jones went on to become a Hollywood fixture. Life is full of unexpected twists in the road at times!

There were also some significant sporting events away from Football:

Japan hosted the Winter Olympics.

In Athletics, Haile Gebrselassie remained unbeaten in 1998 and indeed set four world records.

At Wimbledon, 'Pistol' Pete Sampras won the men's tennis title, whilst Jana Novotna took the ladies' one.

Mark O'Meara took the Golf Open Championship, followed by Vijay Singh taking the US PGA title. It was O'Meara's second Major win of the year.

The Commonwealth Games were held in Kuala Lumpur, Malaysia.

The cycling Tour de France was won by Marco Pantani.

In Formula One, the championship was won by Mika Hakkinen for the first time.

And the New York Yankees won the World Series in baseball.

Arsenal won a closely contested Premier League, with Manchester United finishing in second place. The turning point occurred on 14th March 1998, when Marc Overmars bagged the only goal for Arsenal in the 79th minute of the game held at Old Trafford.

According to the BBC match report, "Arsenal blew the championship race wide open by defeating Manchester United 1- 0 at Old Trafford, which left the Gunners just six points behind United with three games in hand." The BBC report went on to say that "Following their victory over Manchester United, Arsenal's Premiership title odd has been cut from 11/2 to 9/4 by William Hill, who still make United favourites but have lengthened their odds from 1/8 to 1/3."

Arsenal's manager, Arsène Wenger, still thought that the Red Devils were in the driving seat. He told the BBC, "I think United have still got a small advantage because we have to take the points from the games in hand." The match-winner on the day, Marc Overmars, added, "This was a great result for us. But you don't win the Premier League by beating Manchester United; you have to beat the other clubs as well." Overmars was correct—Arsenal won their next eight games on their way to becoming league champions, which was sealed with a 4–0 home win against Everton. Even then, they still had games in hand but would have to settle for winning by just a point as they lost their final two games away at Liverpool and Aston Villa. The margin of victory could have been higher!

It was the first time that a manager had won the league who wasn't from the British Isles. To add insult to injury for United, Arsenal also claimed the FA Cup when they beat Newcastle United in the final. This was the second time that Arsenal had won the domestic double—the first time being way back in the 1970–1971 season. Who can forget the image of Charlie George lying flat out on the Wembley turf on a hot and sunny day?

At the end of the 1997–1998 FA Premier League season, a record total of nine English teams qualified for European competition. Whilst this was good for English football, there was a worrying trend that a gap was forming between the Premier League and the rest of the football pyramid. Arsenal and Manchester United qualified for the Champions League. United would have to negotiate with a potentially tricky pre-qualifying round as they had finished runners-up to the Gunners.

The League Cup was won by Chelsea, who defeated Middleborough also by 2–0 in extra-time. The exact same score as the previous season's FA Cup final involving the same teams and, ultimately, the same winners.

Chelsea completed their own double in that season as they also claimed the European Cup Winners' Cup in Sweden by beating the German team, Stuttgart, by a single goal courtesy of Gianfranco Zola.

So, whilst Arsenal and United would be playing in the prestigious Champions League, the UEFA Cup places went to Liverpool, Leeds United, Aston Villa, and Blackburn Rovers. Chelsea and Newcastle both qualified for the European Cup Winners' Cup: Chelsea, as defending champions, and Newcastle, as runners-up in the FA Cup. The last remaining European space went to Crystal Palace, who qualified for the short-lived Intertoto Cup. Despite finishing bottom of the league, they would qualify through the Fair Play system.

The other teams relegated with Crystal Palace were Bolton and Barnsley. This was to highlight a worrying trend: a gap was forming between England's elite league and the lower leagues. All three had been promoted to the Premier League the previous season, and all three were relegated from it just 12 months later. Had Sunderland not lost the Play-Off final to Charlton Athletic in a dramatic penalty shootout, the 20 teams that would compete in the 1998–1999 season would have been exactly the same as those in the 1996–1997 season.

As well as Charlton making the 'Promised Land' in that legendary shoot-out at Wembley in May 1998, the other two teams promoted via automatic places were Nottingham Forest as First Division champions and Middlesbrough as runners-up.

In Division Two, Graham Taylor's second spell as manager brought instant success as Watford were crowned champions, and the other teams promoted were runners-up, Bristol City, and Grimsby Town, through the play-offs, while Brentford, Plymouth Argyle, Carlisle United, and Southend United were relegated to Division Three.

In Division Three, Notts County won the league and were joined in Division Two by Macclesfield Town, Lincoln City, and the play-off winners, Colchester United. Doncaster Rovers suffered an English League record of 34 defeats and just four wins as they lost their league status. They were replaced by Conference champions, Halifax Town, five years after they had been relegated from the Football League.

Real Madrid claimed the Champions League trophy at the Amsterdam Arena by beating Juventus by a single goal. This was to be Real Madrid's seventh time as champions of Europe, and it was Juventus' third final on the trot.

The UEFA Cup final was an all-Italian affair as Inter Milan beat Lazio by 3–0. This was the first season that the final had not been played over two legs.

In 1998, the world eagerly awaited the FIFA World Cup. It was the 16th World Cup finals and was held in France for the second time, the first being in 1938. France had also hosted the Euros in 1984 and were victorious on home soil, defeating Portugal in a thrilling match that ended 3–2. Sadly, Ireland and the other Home Nations did not even qualify, and as a result, the tournament did not capture the UK's attention.

In 1998, though, both England and Scotland had qualified. Indeed, Scotland kicked off the competition by playing the reigning world champions, Brazil, in Paris. The South Americans came out on top, beating Scotland by 2–1.

Scotland were eliminated in the group stages of the finals after a credible 1–1 draw with Norway, followed by a 3–0 defeat to Morocco.

England did make it through the group stages by beating Tunisia 2–0 and Columbia by the same score, sandwiched between a 2–1 defeat to Romania. England's reward was a Round of 16 clash with Argentina, but the Three Lions went out on penalties. More on this to follow in the next chapter.

As the tournament progressed, the home nation got stronger and stronger, and they reached the final by beating Croatia by 2–1. As they had done in 1994, Brazil also progressed to the final by winning a penalty shoot-out against the Netherlands in the semi-final. The World Cup final was held at the Stade de France in Paris on 12th July 1998, with France winning the game 3–0, with a brace from Zinedine Zidane and an injury-time goal scored by Emmanuel Petit, thus becoming the sixth different nation to be crowned world champions, after Uruguay, Italy, England, West Germany, and Argentina.

However, the real drama occurred before the match when it was announced that Brazil's star player, Ronaldo, would not play in the game. Mystery surrounded as to why he had been pulled from the match, and there was a lot of confusion. This was compounded even further when, just 45 minutes before kick-off, it was announced that Ronaldo was back in the team and would start the game. That news filled in all the conversation pieces in the studios and commentary teams around the globe.

One final note on the World Cup '98 was the sheer number of songs released. Football songs in the 1990s had become a la mode, starting with New Order in 1990 with *World In Motion* and Baddiel and Skinner with the Lightening Seeds in Euro '96 with the also anthemic *Three Lions*. It didn't quite come home for England, but it was close! Indeed, *Three Lions* would get another updated release for the World Cup in France with the imaginative title of *Three Lions '98* by the same artists.

Not to be outdone, Keith Allen (co-writer of *World in Motion*) got together with a cast of (seemingly) thousands to record a song under the pseudonym Fat Les, with a song called *Vindaloo*.

Ever since 1998, these songs have become perpetual bedfellows at every tournament in pubs and clubs up and down the land.

CHAPTER TWO
The Sum of All Its Parts!

"Success depends on your whole team being a single unit"
Pele

***

BEFORE THE 1998–1999 season began, Manchester United announced the parting of ways of two significant players that had played a major part in bringing success to Old Trafford.

Back in 1989, Manchester United purchased Gary Pallister from Middlesborough for £2.3 million, a then-record fee for a defender. Looking back, it is hard to conceive that it was a very difficult time for his new manager, Alex Ferguson, whose stock was at an all-time low. Arriving in 1986 after the World Cup in Mexico, where he had managed the Scotland team, it was expected that he would bring back the glory years quickly. However, it was not to be the case, and silverware kept well away from the Old Trafford trophy cabinet in seasons between 1986 and 1989.

The late, great Jimmy Greaves was sent a letter for one of his newspaper columns during that period, and it received a star award for letter of the week and £10 for the disgruntled fan who had written it. The headline read:

FERGIE MUST GO

The letter read, "The time has come for Manchester United to sack Alex Ferguson. He's been in charge for more than a year and has spent £2 million on new players. Yet the team is now even worse than the one he inherited from Ron Atkinson. United will never win anything while he's the manager."

Jimmy Greaves responded with the following: "Fergie is under pressure, but getting rid of the boss won't solve United's problems. It's the majority of the United team that should get the sack. The club have signed a number of players who should all have done a decent job for the side. But with a couple of notable exceptions, none of them have done the business. They got Atkinson the axe and could do the same for Fergie. They don't have enough pride to play for such a great club as Manchester United."

In many ways, signing the likes of Gary Pallister was a beacon of positivity that soon stopped disgruntled fans from winning 'Star Letters' and financial gain. It's no coincidence that the cleaners were soon to be polishing new silverware when United won the FA Cup in 1990 and then followed it up with the European Cup Winners' Cup in 1991 and the League Cup in 1992. Crystal Palace, Barcelona, and Nottingham Forest were on the receiving end of those victories, respectively.

Pallister's partnership with Steve Bruce was formed straight away, and I think it is fair to say that this was one of the greatest centre-back pairings in English football, not only at United but also in general. In hindsight, Gary Pallister has earned the right to sit with his grandchildren as he regales them with wonder as they request—show us your medals! As well as the three trophies already mentioned, Pallister also won the following:

Four Premier Leagues, two more FA Cups, five Charity Shields, and one European Super Cup.

File Gary Pallister into the 'legends' section of the Manchester United history books. So, it came to pass that in 1998 he re-signed for the Middlesborough for even more money than United had purchased him for—and at the age of 33! File that under the 'shrewd' section.

The other notable departure was Brian McClair, who had swapped the green of Glasgow for the red of Manchester back in 1987, where he stayed for 11 years. Negotiations between Manchester United and Celtic had originally seen a significant difference in valuation. United had offered £400,000, miles away from Celtic's asking price of £2 million. If that had been met, it would have made McClair the most expensive British player at the time. In the end, the fee was agreed at £850,000. Manchester United had gotten themselves a bargain as it turned out—and an instant one at that. In his first season, 1987–1988, McClair got himself on the scoresheet 31 times in all competitions. However, McClair found goals harder to come by the following year, although he still managed 16 in all competitions. The limelight was somewhat stolen with the return of the 'Prodigal Son'—Mark Hughes.

When United won the FA Cup in 1990, although it was Lee Martin who took the plaudits for scoring the winning goal in the final replay, McClair's contributions on the road to Wembley were undeniable as he bagged goals in the fifth round, quarter-final and semi-final.

A similar pattern occurred in the 1990–1991 season as Manchester United went on to win the European Cup Winners' Cup as a result of winning the FA Cup in the previous campaign, with McClair scoring goals in every round except for the final, when a brace from Mark Hughes defeated Barcelona. McClair did manage to score in a final eventually, when United beat Forest in the Rumbelows Cup final. He was no longer the cup final bridesmaid!

Upon the arrival of a certain Mr. Cantona in 1992, McClair found himself playing in midfield, a position he adapted well to. Premier League titles soon followed, and he scored the final goal in the 1994 FA Cup final, a 4–0 rout of Chelsea. Overall, Choccy (McClair's nickname at United) played for Manchester United on 355 occasions and scored 88 goals.

Other players that left Old Trafford either before or during the 1998–1999 season were: Grant Brebner, Chris Casper, Ben Thornley, Kevin Pilkington, Graeme Tomlinson, Erik Nevland, Ronnie Wallwork, Danny Higginbotham, Jordi Cruyff, Michael Twiss, and Alex Notman. It's not so easy to replace players who had contributed to so much success in the past. The selection process needed to be spot on with little margin for error if they were to take pole position back from Arsenal.

United would break transfer records twice in order to achieve it.

Jaap Stam had caught the eye of many people, not least Alex Ferguson, as he helped Holland reach the semi-final of the 1998

World Cup. He was a towering and imposing centre-half, and in the mind of Ferguson, he was the perfect replacement for the departing Gary Pallister. United paid PSV £10.6 million for Stam's services.

Big things were expected of the giant Dutchman. However, it didn't start too well for Stam in his very first few games as a United player, but it soon became very apparent that the positives of Jaap Stam far outweighed the negatives, as he formed formidable partnerships with either Ronny Johnsen, Henning Berg, or David May.

Alex Ferguson made no secret that he was an admirer of the prolific Aston Villa striker, Dwight Yorke, and indeed had referenced him as Villa's main threat a few seasons earlier, when United had drawn at Villa Park in the 1996–1997 season.

Yorke had been spotted playing football on a beach in Trinidad and Tobago when Villa were on tour there in 1989. Mainly a bit part player until Brian Little arrived in 1994, Yorke flourished under Little's tenure and was on the scoresheet when Villa beat Leeds United in the 1996 Coca-Cola Cup final. Yorke was becoming hot property, and rumours were abounding in the early summer of 1998 that United were interested in signing him. Despite the rumour mill going into overdrive, Yorke was named in the starting line-up for Villa's first game of the 1998–1999 season—a goalless draw to Everton. Shortly after that match, Yorke submitted an official transfer request, such was his desire to ply his trade with United. This prompted a now famous flippant quote from the Villa Manager at the time, John Gregory: "If I had a gun, I would have shot him." The question, "Will he, won't he sign?" was a protracted one and filled a lot of column inches in the newspapers until Yorke finally signed for United for a reported fee of £12.6 million on 28th August 1998. He had scored freely in the claret and blue of Aston Villa and was about to do the same in the red of Manchester United!

Sandwiched in between the two big money transfers (although considerable in its own right) was the signing of Jesper Blomqvist. Although he wasn't to figure in as many games as the others, his trickery on the left-hand side was there for all to see. The Swede was purchased from Italian side Parma for

£4.4 million in July 1998 and made his full debut in the 4–1 home win against Charlton in early September.

The trio of arrivals joined a squad brimming with talent, including one David Beckham. Beckham had come to prominence in the 1995–1996 season when United had won the double, but it wasn't until the first game of the following season that people really started to sit up and take notice. It was a sunny day in August 1996, and United were playing Wimbledon at Selhurst Park. The Dons were ground-sharing with Crystal Palace at the time. In the 90th minute, Beckham picked the ball up on the halfway line, looked up to see the Wimbledon goalkeeper, Neil Sullivan, off his line, and then proceeded to ping the ball past Sullivan with pin-point precision into the back of the net. Arms raised—and with the trademark Beckham grin—the football world had found a new icon. Brand Beckham began. "It changed my life," said a fresh-faced Beckham of his wonder goal. "The ball seemed to be in the air for hours and it all went quiet. Then the ball went in and it just erupted." David Beckham became the advertising world's best friend after that day; he was good looking as well as being a very talented footballer. When he started dating Victoria Adams (Posh Spice in the Spice Girls) they became the dream team and media darlings.

So, it came as no surprise when Beckham was picked by Glenn Hoddle to be a part of his England team for the World Cup in France in 1998.

On 30th June, at the home of Saint Etienne, England were paired against Argentina in the Round of 16. The first half started at a blistering pace. Two penalties converted by both teams in the first 10 minutes set down a marker for what was to come. Firstly, Gabriel Batistuta on the sixth minute, and then just four minutes later, Alan Shearer put England back in the game. Then Liverpool's boy wonder, Michael Owen, scored a brilliant goal as he waltzed through the Argentine defence to give England a 2–1 lead. That lead lasted until the stroke of half-time, when Javier Zanetti levelled with virtually the last kick of the half. It was all-square, and all to play for. However, just two minutes into the second-half, the game was changed on its head when Diego Simone challenged Beckham to a 50/50 ball. It was fairly obvious at the time that the foul had been committed by Simone as Beckham fell to the floor. Whilst on the floor, Beckham kicked out at Simone, striking his calf, in full view of the referee, Kim Melton Nelson of Denmark. The Argentina players were quick to remind the referee that this action from Beckham was worthy of a red card, and seconds later, Beckham received his marching orders. Gabriel Batistuta stood there, nodding his approval. England were down to 10 men and crashed out of the World Cup, losing to the South Americans in a penalty shootout. The media and indeed the nation needed a scapegoat, and it was to be David Beckham. Unfortunately, Beckham quickly became persona non grata and the most hated man in the country. *The Daily Mirror's* headline the following day read:

10 HEROIC LIONS—ONE STUPID BOY

A few days later, the same newspaper printed a dartboard on its front page with a picture of Beckham in the bull's eye, with the headline:

STILL BITTER?
TAKE YOUR FURY OUT ON OUR
DAVID BECKHAM DARTBOARD

The Daily Mail's headlines were a little more sober:

MOMENT OF LUNANCY THAT COST CUP HOPES

David Beckham appeared to be public enemy number one for many weeks and months to come, and the inevitable death threats began to emerge. Another newspaper column from Jimmy Greaves read, "David Beckham has quite simply got to go and play abroad now. If he stays here, it could destroy him." At least there was no dartboard with that article!

Most telling, and also most disturbing, was the effigy that was burned in United's first away game of the season at Upton Park, the then-home of West Ham United.

Beckham would reflect on this time many years later on ITV whilst supporting the Duke of Cambridge to promote a

'Mentally Healthy Culture' in football. "I made a mistake, you know; I made a mistake in 1998, and the reaction was pretty brutal. I was constantly criticised on the pitch verbally. But I was lucky. I had a support system in Manchester United, and the manager, and obviously family."

It was great to hear that Beckham received support from his family and the football club, but for me, the most striking part of his statement was the manager's role. Alex Ferguson had a somewhat island mentality when it came to protecting his players. One only has to think of how he dealt with Eric Cantona after his infamous kung-fu kick on a fan in 1995 for further proof. Another example is Ferguson not allowing the media to speak to Ryan Giggs until he was 20. That was exactly what David Beckham needed—to be surrounded and protected by Alex Ferguson and the club in general. Ferguson even selected Beckham to play in the pre-season friendlies after the time off from World Cup duties. Phil Neville recalled, "The rewards for Manchester United were swift. It would take a little longer in an England shirt, but it would still happen."

Beckham was part of the Class of '92, a band of very special young players that won the FA Youth Cup (under the guidance of Eric Harrison) in that year and then went on to serve the first team so well for the rest of the 1990s. As well as Beckham, the group consisted of Gary Neville, Phil Neville, Nicky Butt, Paul Scholes, and Ryan Giggs. They soon became known as "Fergie's Fledglings."

In 1998, they were no longer Fledglings but, moreover, they were flourishing. Beckham had replaced Andrei Kanchelskis on the right-hand side of midfield, and Nicky Butt had replaced Paul Ince in the centre of it. Butt had made the step up to the senior team during the 1992–1993 season as a substitute in a Premier League game against Oldham Athletic, a game in which United won by 3–0.

During the course of the next few seasons, Butt would find himself in the first team, starting games and scoring many important goals in the process. In the 1997–1998 season, Butt found himself as a direct replacement for Roy Keane when the Irishman was side-lined for much of the start of that campaign. Such was his effectiveness in Keane's role, Butt made the PFA Team of the Year for that season.

Gary Neville had made the right-back place his own since the 1994–1995 season, when he replaced the experienced Paul Parker. Neville joined the club as an apprentice upon leaving school in 1991 and made his first team debut against Torpedo Moscow in the UEFA Cup during the 1992–1993 season. Neville was a driven character who was aggressive and dedicated to the cause—not only for United but also for England. He really was a true club man, not just because he was a Manchester United supporter, but moreover, because he never plied his trade for any other club. His partnership with David Beckham on the right-hand side of the pitch paid dividends on many occasions.

On the left-hand side, and opposite Gary Neville, was Dennis Irwin. Ferguson had acquired the Republic of Ireland left-back from Oldham Athletic in the summer of 1990. Irwin soon found himself as a stalwart in the team and served United superbly, so much so that Alex Ferguson remarked that "pound for pound, Irwin was my greatest signing." At the dawn of the 1998–1999 season, Irwin was just a few months off his 33rd birthday, and knocking at his door was Phil Neville, the younger brother of Gary. Like his brother, he went on to represent his country at senior level many times. Phil Neville could also play in midfield, he offered versatility.

Paul Scholes made his debut for the senior team in the 1994–1995 season. It was a memorable match; not only for the skills, vison, and intelligence that he displayed, but because he scored both goals in a 2–1 win over Port Vale in the League Cup. He made his debut in the league just a few days later, and whilst United went on to lose 3–2 against Ipswich Town, Scholes found himself on the scoresheet once again. Scholes really came into his own during the 1995–1996 season when he was presented with more first-team opportunities as Mark Hughes moved to Chelsea. With Hughes' departure and Eric Cantona serving a lengthy suspension, Scholes partnered Andy Cole upfront and took the opportunity with both hands. Scholes went on to score 14 goals for United during the 1995–1996 campaign and never looked back. Like Gary Neville, he was a true club man himself as he would only represent Manchester United at club level.

Ryan Giggs was a major part of the Class of '92, although he had stolen a march on the rest by making his debut against

Everton on 2nd March 1991, replacing Dennis Irwin in a 2–0 defeat. The young Giggs would not be part of United's squad for the European Cup Winners' Cup final success against Barcelona in the May of that year—Lee Sharpe was given the left-wing berth for the final, with Danny Wallace on the bench. However, disappointing it must have been for Giggs, he did become a regular in the 1991–1992 campaign as United finished runners-up to Leeds United. He was voted the PFA Young Player of the Year and also set up Brian McClair for the winning goal in the League Cup victory against Nottingham Forest at Wembley.

Leeds United were the last team to win the old First Division before the Premier League began, and during 1992–1993 Giggs flourished as he made the left-wing his own, relegating Lee Sharpe to the bench. At the end of the year, he had won his first Premier League winner's medal and was voted the PFA Young Player of the Year once more. He followed this up with another Premier League title as well as his first FA Cup winner's medal in 1994. He was injured for the first half of the 1994–1995 season but was back in action for the second Premier League and FA Cup double win which was in 1995–1996. By the start of the 1998–1999 season, and at just 24 years of age, Giggs had contributed greatly to United's success under Ferguson. The worrying thing for English and European defences was that he was still just coming into his prime.

Roy Keane had shaved his hair off prior to the start of the season, and if his doubters thought that his haircut would have the same effect as it had on Samson, then they were soon to be disappointed. Keane had been purchased by Manchester United from Nottingham Forest in the summer of 1993 for a then-record fee between English clubs of £3.75 million. Keane was simply a winner, and the ultimate box-to-box midfielder, in the mould of Bryan Robson, who had made this position his own in the 1980s. As befits a warrior like Keane, he would spend time out with injuries and suspensions during the 1997–1998 season, and one wonders if United would have squandered an 11-point lead in the same manner if Keane had been on the pitch, especially as he had been made captain due to the unexpected retirement of Eric Cantona in the same season. Little did he know at the start of August 1998 what was to come in the next nine months or so, and the impact he would have, especially on a balmy night in Turin later in the season.

Up front, Dwight Yorke joined the ranks with Andy Cole, Teddy Sheringham, and Ole Gunnar Solskjaer, a formidable foursome to choose from. What isn't commonly known is that Solskjaer nearly joined Tottenham Hotspur for £5.5 million, and Andy Cole was originally offered to Aston Villa as a makeshift in the Yorke transfer. Both stayed, and both would have no regrets! Apparently, Solskjaer was called into Ferguson's office and was told that a deal had been reached between Martin Edwards and Alan Sugar. Ferguson had told Solskjaer that he didn't want him to leave and that he would feature in the team, and Solskjaer agreed not to pursue the move. In fairness, he didn't want to leave the club anyway.

Whilst the relationship on the field between Dwight Yorke and Andy Cole took some time to develop (mainly because they were not really paired straight away), their off-field relationship blossomed very quickly. Yorke would visit Cole at his home and eat with the family. Cole acted in an advisory capacity, somewhat similar to Yorke in the early days, and was happy to afford Yorke his time in matters such as the best places to live and the best restaurants and shops to visit.

Peter Schmeichel was a man with things on his mind in 1998. The Danish goalkeeper had been at Old Trafford since 1991. To say that he was a safe pair of hands during that time is doing the great Dane a total disservice. In the 1992–1993 season, he ensured that the ball did not hit the back of his net at all during 23 competitive games. Widely regarded as the best goalkeeper in the world in the 1990s, Schmeichel's medal tally was impressive to say the least—at international level as well as domestically. Denmark didn't even qualify for the European Championships in Sweden in 1992, finishing second to Yugoslavia in the group qualifying stages. However, due to the troubles in Yugoslavia, UEFA decided that they could not compete, and Denmark, as runners-up in the group, were invited to take their place in the tournament. Incredibly, little-fancied Denmark actually went on to win the competition beating Germany 2–0 in the final. It wouldn't be the first time that Schmeichel would claim to be a champion of Europe during the decade.

The 1998–1999 season didn't start off well for Manchester United's number one. Three goals conceded against Arsenal at Wembley in the Charity Shield and a further two against Leicester City in the first home game of the season led to the media questioning whether Schmeichel's outstanding career was coming to an end. Concerns were raised that age was catching up with him—he would turn 35 in November 1998. However, as always, he received public backing from Alex Ferguson: "He's a fine goalkeeper. The best I have ever had and the best Manchester United have ever had. Sometimes people are going to make mistakes, because otherwise they think you are flawless." He added, "But people wouldn't be human if they didn't make mistakes. There have been very few from Peter during his time here, and they have been certainly outweighed by the number of marvellous performances he has contributed to." Alex Ferguson was well aware that Peter Schmeichel would be playing his very last season for the club because Schmeichel had decided that after seven glorious years, it was time for a change. It was eventually announced in November that he was leaving the club. The only other person to know this was Martin Edwards. Perhaps keeping the secret played on his mind more than he knew it would and it affected his early performances in 1998–1999, but maybe it was also a relief for Schmeichel because what happened after the announcement was nothing short of sporting excellence.

In 1998, Alex Ferguson was happy with Manchester United's arrivals and departure lounges. He had at least two players for every position in his squad, and he knew that whoever played and whoever deputised would meet his required standards mentally and physically. Mixed with the talent and temperament as well, Sir Alex was confident that they would rise to the occasion and savour the challenges that they would face in the next nine months.

There would also be significant changes in Alex Ferguson's management team that occurred during the season, with Brian Kidd moving on. In 1968, on his 19th birthday, Kidd had been part of the Manchester United team that won the European Cup at Wembley. He actually scored one of the goals in that famous 4–1 victory over Benfica in the final under Sir Matt Busby. All in all, he scored 52 goals and played over 200 times for the club. His career would also take him to clubs such as Arsenal, Manchester City, Everton, and Bolton Wanderers before plying his trade in the MSL for several American clubs. He hung up his boots in 1984, having played in well over 500 games and scoring over 200 goals. He also made a couple of appearances for England in senior matches and scored a single goal.

Football ran through the veins of Brian Kidd, who was born in Manchester, and it came as no surprise that he would end up in management at some point after the boots were hung up. The opportunity would come soon enough when he began his coaching career at Barrow before briefly managing Preston North End for several games in 1986. It was all part of his learning the trade from the touchline, and in 1988, Kidd returned to Old Trafford as a youth team coach. Over the next three years, Kidd would oversee the development of a host of talented players, like Ryan Giggs and Darren Ferguson. A vacancy as assistant manager to Alex Ferguson opened up when Archie Knox moved to Rangers in the summer of 1991, and he seized the opportunity to step up and make his mark. He helped Ferguson guide United to a League Cup win in 1992, the Premier League title in 1993, the double in 1994 and again in 1996, as well as another Premier League title in 1997. It was a formidable partnership, but the cracks had started to appear in the summer of 1998 when Kidd questioned why Ferguson wanted to bring in Dwight Yorke from Villa. That angered Ferguson somewhat, and it was perhaps time for Kidd to manage his own club, so he took up the reins at Blackburn Rovers in December 1998. Blackburn had been struggling at the foot of the table prior to Kidd's arrival, and he was not able to keep Rovers up as they crashed out of the Premier League just four years after they had been crowned champions.

It had been a massively successful time for United, and Alex Ferguson would need to make sure that his next assistant would hit the ground running and fit in straight away with the ethos of the club and the fact that it was involved in several major competitions. For now, though, Jim Ryan would take the role on an interim basis until a new appointment was made. The media and the fans pondered who would be coming in, with many speculating that the appointment would be a high-profile one from either England or one of the top leagues in Europe.

No one could have foreseen that the appointment would be somewhat lower-key, and this is exactly what happened when Steve McClaren took up the post vacated by Brian Kidd very early in 1999. McClaren's playing career was very different from the one that Kidd had experienced. McClaren had made his professional debut in 1979 for Hull City before playing in midfield for Derby County, Lincoln City, Bristol City, and Oxford United. A lower-league servant who hung up his boots in 1992. After retiring from playing, the lad from Fulford in York began his coaching career as a youth and reserve team coach at Oxford United, where Denis Smith was manager. McClaren then moved back to Derby County in 1995, where he was assistant manager to Jim Smith. This proved to be an invaluable time for McClaren as he was learning from one of the most astute and experienced managers in Jim Smith, who was affectionately known as the Bald Eagle. Derby County were to enjoy the fruits of the Premier League as they were promoted the following season and established themselves as a top-flight team.

Alex Ferguson had been taking notes and decided that McClaren would become his number two at Old Trafford. He decided to make his move after United had played Derby County, and it was all systems go once Jim Smith had agreed to let Fergie talk to his assistant. It happened very quickly, and Steve McClaren described it as a "whirlwind." Not everyone at United had heard of Derby's assistant manager, though, especially those located in the boardroom. Martin Edwards had introduced him as "Steve McClaridge," perhaps a hybrid of McClaren and the much-travelled striker, Steve Claridge! Either way, it caused a few raised eyebrows and smirks at the time. It was soon to be forgotten, though, as McClaren proved that he was the right man for the job, and he took to it like a duck to water. It may have been a massive step up for McClaren, but he made an instant impact. The trepidation that some players may have had after Brian Kidd's departure soon dissipated. The players saw McClaren's vision as being different from what they had experienced previously, and in many ways, it was very refreshing.

Alex Ferguson had once again made a brave decision that

was soon to be vindicated. A juxtaposition in terms of methods and ideals between two different coaches and a team of players willing to adapt to the changes. That could only be a good thing.

The squad had been assembled. These were the players that Alex Ferguson had faith in to deliver for the 1998–1999 season:

Goalkeepers

Raimond van der Gouw
Born: Oldenzaal, Holland, 24th March 1963
Senior United Debut: v Aston Villa (A) Premier League. 21st September 1996

Peter Schmeichel
Born: Gladsaxe Municipality, Denmark, 18th November 1963
Senior United Debut: v Notts County (H) Division One, 17th August 1991

Nick Culkin
Born: York, 6th July 1978
Senior United Debut: v Arsenal (A) Premier League, 22nd August 1999

Defenders

Henning Berg
Born: Eidsvoll, Norway, 1st September 1969
Senior United Debut: v Southampton (H) Premier League, 13th August 1997

Wes Brown
Born: Manchester, 13th October 1979
Senior United Debut: v Leeds (H) Premier League, 4th May 1998

Michael Clegg
Born: Ashton-under-Lyne, 3rd July 1977
Senior United Debut: v Middlesbrough (A) Premier League, 23rd November 1996

John Curtis
Born: Nuneaton, 3rd September 1978
Senior United Debut: v Ipswich Town (A) League Cup, 14th October 1997

Danny Higginbotham
Born: Manchester, 29th December 1978
Senior United Debut: v Barnsley (A) Premier League, 10th May 1998

Dennis Irwin
Born: Cork, 31st October 1965
Senior United Debut: v Coventry City (H) Division One, 15th August 1990

Ronny Johnsen
Born: Sandefjord, Norway, 10th June 1969
Senior United Debut: v Wimbledon (A) Premier League, 17th August 1996

David May
Born: Oldham, 24th June 1970
Senior United Debut: v Queens Park Rangers (H) Premier League, 10th August 1994

Gary Neville
Born: Bury, 18th February 1975
Senior United Debut: v Torpedo Moscow (H) UEFA Cup, 16th September 1992

Phil Neville
Born: Bury, 21st January 1977
Senior United Debut: v Wrexham (H) FA Cup, 28th January 1995

Jaap Stam
Born: Kampen, Holland, 17th July 1972
Senior United Debut: v Arsenal (N) FA Charity Shield, 9th August 1998

Ronnie Wallwork
Born: Manchester, 10th September 1977
Senior United Debut: v Barnsley (H) Premier League, 25th October 1997

Midfielders

David Beckham
Born: Leytonstone, 2nd May 1975
Senior United Debut: v Brighton (A) League Cup, 23rd September 1992

Nicky Butt
Born: Manchester, 21st January 1975
Senior United Debut: v Oldham Athletic (H) Premier League, 21st November 1992

Jonathan Greening
Born: Scarborough, 2nd Jan 1979
Senior United Debut: v Bury (H) League Cup, 28th October 1998

Roy Keane
Born: Cork, 10th August 1971
Senior United Debut: v Norwich City (A) Premier League, 15th August 1993

Paul Scholes
Born: Salford, 16th November 1974
Senior United Debut: v Port Vale (A) League Cup, 21st November 1994

Michael Twiss
Born: Salford, 26th December 1977
Senior United Debut: v Barnsley (A) FA Cup, 25th February 1998

Mark Wilson
Born: Scunthorpe, 9th February 1979
Senior United Debut: v Brondby (A) UEFA Champions League, 25th February 1998

Forwards

Jesper Blomqvist
Born: Tavelsjo, Sweden, 5th February 1974
Senior United Debut: v Charlton Athletic (H) Premier League, 9th September 1998

Andy Cole
Born: Nottingham, 15th October 1971
Senior United Debut: v Blackburn Rovers (H) Premier League, 22nd January 1995

Jordi Cruyff
Born: Amsterdam, Holland, 9th February 1974
Senior United Debut: v Wimbledon (A) Premier League, 17th August 1996

Ryan Giggs
Born: Cardiff, 29th November 1973
Senior United Debut: v Everton (H) Division One, 2nd March 1991

Erik Nevland
Born: Stavanger, Norway, 10th November 1977
Senior United Debut: v Ipswich Town (A) League Cup, 14th October 1997

Alex Notman
Born: Edinburgh, 10th December 1979
Senior United Debut: v Tottenham Hotspur (A) League Cup, 2nd December 1998

Teddy Sheringham
Born: Highams Park, 2nd April 1966
Senior United Debut: v Tottenham Hotspur (A) Premier League, 10th August 1997

Ole Gunnar Solskjaer
Born: Kristiansund, Norway, 26th February 1973
Senior United Debut: v Blackburn Rovers (H) Premier League, 25th August 1996

Dwight Yorke
Born: Canaan, Trinidad and Tobago, 3rd November 1971
Senior United Debut: v West Ham United (A) Premier League, 22nd August 1998

CHAPTER THREE
Red or Dead—Game 1

"It's like that, and that's the way it is!"
Run DMC

***

Sunday 9th August 1998
FA Charity Shield

Arsenal 3 Manchester United 0
Wembley Stadium
Attendance: 67,342
Referee: Graham Poll

Arsenal: Seaman, Dixon, Adams, Keown, Winterburn, Parlour, Vieira, Petit, Overmars, Bergkamp, Anelka—Substitutes: Bould, Boa Morte, Hughes, Manninger, Vivas, Wreh, Grimandi.

Manchester United: Schmeichel, Neville (G), Johnsen, Stam, Irwin, Beckham, Keane, Butt, Giggs, Scholes, Cole—Substitutes: Berg, Solskjaer, Cruyff, Neville (P), Sheringham, Culkin, May.

***

THE FIRST OF THE 63 games that Manchester United would play during the 1998–1999 season took place on 9th August 1998, on a sweltering hot day at Wembley. It was the traditional season curtain-raiser, otherwise known as the Charity Shield (now Community Shield.) Arsenal went into the game as reigning

Premier League champions and FA Cup holders, while United had added nothing to their trophy cabinet the previous year. The Manchester United fans at Wembley, and those watching it at home, were still smarting from the eight points capitulation at the hands of the Gunners in the previous season, and there was trepidation as to whether the Red Devil's best days were behind them. Up to that point, no team had challenged United's '90s dominance like Arsene Wenger's side had, and it felt like there was a real threat emerging from North London.

A positive for Manchester United was the return of a shaven-headed Roy Keane. The Irishman had not played competitive football for almost a year after he damaged his knee ligaments in an infamous game against Leeds United at Elland Road. United fans would also get to see Jaap Stam for the first time in action. Manchester United dominated the early part of the game, but Arsenal took the game to their closest rivals and looked fitter, stronger, and sharper. United could not use the excuse that their players were tired after the World Cup because Arsenal also had representatives at the tournament, two of whom had even played in the final.

United fan, Dilardo Parhbga, shares his experience from attending the game. He had travelled down to London the day before the match and stopped at the nearby Wembley Hotel. He had been out for a few beers on the Saturday night, but was unsure what part of London he'd been to and couldn't remember how he got back to his hotel. The geographical situation worsened for him and his pals after the match. They tried to leave the capital only to get on the wrong underground line! Perhaps it would have been better for him to have found himself lost before the game! Dilardo takes up the story, "We got back home just in time for last orders at our local, wondering what the effect of the previous season and that day's result would have on the oncoming season."

Another United fan, Darren Keighley, was celebrating his birthday on the day of the match. Darren and his mates had boarded a National Express coach at 6 am, armed with bags of beer. The assistant coach driver took an instant dislike to him and his group of mates, so they had decided to call him Blakey (from the ITV comedy show *On the Buses*) and reminded him frequently of his new name all the way from Manchester to the capital. Darren continues, "The seats we had at Wembley were awful as we had a post in front of us. We got beat, and it put a right dampener on my celebrations. After the match, we decided to get the late coach back to Manchester so we could continue the drinking around Wembley. One bar in particular would not let us in as we had our football tops on. We were told that we could get in if we took them off, so in we went topless! We had a great time."

The media could see the potential swing in power as well as United fans. Oliver Holt reported on the match for *The Times*: "Arsenal turned the FA Charity Shield into a giant housewarming party yesterday as they settled comfortably into the venue that will house their Champions League ties by embarrassing their invited guests, Manchester United, and adding another Wembley triumph to their FA Cup final victory here last May. Quite what the significance of their 3–0 win over Alex Ferguson's side holds is difficult to judge. In the second half, in particular, United appeared to be playing with the European Cup qualifying round tie against LKS Lodz on Wednesday in mind, conserving their energy, [and] withdrawing their leading players from the fray en masse, but the emphatic nature of Arsenal's win, against the team that they overhauled so dramatically in the league last season, can only leave them in good heart as they prepare to open the defence of their FA Carling Premiership title against Nottingham Forest a week today, and United harbouring doubts about their ability to wrest the trophy back."

Holt went on, "Both teams have been engaged in fruitless searches for a new striker over the summer, and, on this showing, United's need appears to be the more pressing. Andy Cole hardly mustered a shot, and the suspicion is returning that United will not be able to conquer Europe with him leading the line. Things will improve when Roy Keane gets closer to full fitness, but, if nothing else, the game yesterday proved that United have more work to do than Arsenal to ready themselves for the marathon ahead."

Ferguson said, "You can learn certain things from the games we played on our pre-season tour of Scandinavia, but that was a real match today. I thought it was very competitive and that we matched them for much of the first half. Those of us, though, who had imagined that Arsenal might have felt sluggish under the accumulated weight of the laurel wreaths that have hung around their necks. French World Cup winners Emmanuel Petit and Patrick Vieira, in particular, might have been sated with honours but were mistaken"

Roy Keane wasn't taking any prisoners, and it was hard to believe that the battling midfielder had been out of the team through his injuries as he showed no signs of uncertainty in his play. There were no real clear-cut chances in the opening exchanges, with both teams looking composed and not wishing to give anything away. United had the best chance when Scholes was denied by David Seaman. However, as the first half grew, Arsenal started to dominate the game, and they took the lead in the 33rd minute after some great interlink play between Viera, Bergkamp, and Anelka. United seemed to clear the chance that had been created, but the clearance from Johnsen was blocked by the advancing Anelka into the path of Marc Overmars, who put the ball high into the United goal.

No more goals were scored in the first half, and the advantage was firmly with the team from North London. Arsenal continued the stamping of authority on the match in the second half, proving that their dominance in the previous season was something they were not prepared to let go of. Christopher Wreh had come on for Dennis Bergkamp and extended Arsenal's lead after Peter Schmeichel had blocked his first attempt, and a firm victory was confirmed when Nicholas Anelka ran onto a pass from Ray Parlour, who evaded the hapless Jaap Stam to fire in the third. Game over.

"Winning things is a good habit," Wenger said. "I don't think winning today will help us to beat Manchester United in the league, but at least the players know where they stand a bit more now. Psychologically, it was important for us to win at Wembley, so we feel happy here during the Champions League."

CHAPTER FOUR
Red or Dead—Game 3

"Winning things is a good habit"
Arsène Wenger

***

Saturday 15th August 1998
FA Carling Premiership

Manchester United 2 Leicester City 2
Old Trafford
Attendance: 55,052
Referee: Neale Barry

Manchester United: Schmeichel, Neville (G), Irwin, Keane, Johnsen, Stam, Beckham, Butt, Cole, Scholes, Giggs—Substitutes: May, Sheringham, Neville (P), Berg, Culkin.

Leicester City: Keller, Savage, Sinclair, Elliot, Walsh, Izzet, Lennon, Zagorakis, Heskey, Cottee, Guppy—Substitutes: Taggart, Parker, Kåmark, Arphexad, Wilson.

***

THE FIRST HOME game of the season has been chosen as a 'Red or Dead' game and is worthy of a chapter for several reasons. Not only was it the first game in the league, but it also served to take note of just how much Manchester United would simply not lie down and have their tummy tickled; they played to the final whistle.

David Beckham was in a pensive mood as United took to the field on a boiling hot and sunny day. On his mind was how he was going to be treated after what had happened in the World Cup a few weeks before, but he needn't have worried. The Old Trafford faithful were in unison and solidarity, singing his name.

On paper at least, it was likely Leicester City who would provide a sterner test to United after the relative ease of the Champions League home tie against Lodz, a few days earlier. Martin O'Neil had built a good and solid squad that could hold its own in the Premier League. The Foxes had won the League Cup in 1996–1997, which was made even more remarkable as they had only just been promoted in the previous season. They also achieved two consecutive top 10 finishes.

The sterner test on paper did in fact transpire onto the pitch.

It's fair to say that the new central defensive partnership of Stam and Johnsen was still in its forming stage, and Leicester capitalised on this as early as the 7th minute. Muzzy Izzet crossed the ball for Emile Heskey, who scored from close range. The United fans in the ground could be forgiven for thinking that they had not quite recovered from the mauling at the hands of Arsenal the previous week at Wembley.

Leicester had come out of the blocks quicker and stronger and could have easily extended their lead through Tony Cottee, who could have scored a brace before half-time.

The end of the first half drew welcome relief for Manchester United, although this would be the end of Jaap Stam's involvement as he was replaced by Henning Berg at the interval. The second half started in a similar fashion. United were simply not at the races, and it came as no surprise when Cottee finally got on the scoresheet with 14 minutes to go to double the Foxes' lead. Leicester had beaten United at Old Trafford the season before, so their lead came as no real surprise to the fans.

However, the Old Trafford side then became the Manchester United that we would see time and time again over the next nine months. Around 30 years earlier, back in 1968, Elvis Presley made his comeback dressed in black leather—and it was spectacular. United were about to do the same over and over again, albeit on a different stage and in red, not black —and not in leather either!

In the 79th minute, Teddy Sheringham (on for Gary Neville) reduced the deficit as he nudged home David Beckham's shot that was going wide. Becks would get on the scoresheet himself and salvage an unlikely point for the home team deep in stoppage time. It was a beautiful 30-yard free-kick that soared over the Leicester wall and into the back of the net. The Leicester fans had not been as supportive of the Londoner as the home fans had been. A huge understatement as the abuse was non-stop from the start to the finish. It was a great moment for Beckham to savour as the free kick was right in front of the Leicester fans. The right-sided midfielder made his feelings known to the away fans, and who could blame him? In his 2003 autobiography, *My Side*, Beckham says that all he wanted to do when he scored that goal was to turn around to every United fan and thank them for being on his side.

Those fans were on his side, this would not always be the case when playing away in front of partisan home crowds as witnessed at West Ham United a week later. But being in front of the home fans, made Becks feel good again, and it was all that he needed to know—he already knew that he had the club and players on his side. Phil Neville once described the club: "Man United is great. Once you go through the doors of the training ground, it's almost like you're behind the Berlin Wall and nobody can touch you."

The *Manchester Evening News* correspondent at that time was Stuart Mathieson. His report from the opening league match started with the abuse that David Beckham had received since the World Cup Finals during the summer: "The World Cup has a lot to answer for as far as Manchester United are concerned—but payback time has begun. England's 21-day June sojourn in France was damaging for some Old Trafford reputations. None more so than David Beckham. He was the focal point of one of the most controversial incidents in England's tournament. Beckham's initial axing from the opening World Cup line-up provided many column inches of debate. Ultimately, it was to prove nothing in comparison to the word mileage following his red card against Argentina. Much of this was given over to the possibility that the aftermath of Saint-Etienne may hound him out of the country."

Mathieson also pointed out that Teddy Sheringham had

received some ill-comment inches in the national newspapers, almost demanding that the England manager, Glenn Hoddle, took Michael Owen over the more experienced talisman. In the end, that was exactly what happened, and some could say it was justified, especially in that game against Argentina. But Sheringham's reputation had taken a knock and that was unfair.

Whilst the vitriol suffered by Beckham was far more than that suffered by Sheringham, it was still rewarding for Alex Ferguson and the fans to see both players on the scoresheet. Old wounds would soon heal. Beckham, in particular, was thankful for all of the support he had received on the opening day of the league campaign, but he knew he wouldn't have the backing of the opposition fans and possibly England fans as well—at least in the short term anyway.

Old Trafford had taken a deep breath, held it for a few seconds, and then breathed out again against the Foxes from Leicester. It was a game that they drew, looked likely to lose, and was one of those matches that almost felt like a win. After that match, Alex Ferguson admitted that it was debatable whether his team had deserved a point in the end. He wasn't wrong, but they had got the point, and that was the main thing. Ferguson said, "We're a little behind in our preparations. We will get better."

He wasn't wrong!

CHAPTER FIVE
Red or Dead—Game 6

"When you're smiling."
Joe Goodwin, Larry Shay, Mark Fisher

***

Wednesday 9th September 1998
FA Carling Premiership

Manchester United 4 Charlton Athletic 1
Old Trafford
Attendance: 55,147
Referee: Paul Durkin

Manchester United: Schmeichel, Neville (P), Irwin, Keane, Johnsen, Stam, Beckham, Scholes, Solskjaer, Yorke, Blomqvist— Substitutes: Cole, Sheringham, van der Gouw, Berg, Wilson.

Charlton Athletic: Ilic, Mills, Powell, Redfearn, Brown, Youds, Newton, Kinsella, Hunt, Mendonca, Robinson—Substitutes: Petterson, Jones (K), Mortimer, Jones (S), Balmer.

***

THE VISIT OF newly promoted Charlton Athletic was significant on a number of levels. Firstly, it was United's first league win of the new season, and a comprehensive one at that. Dwight Yorke and Jesper Blomqvist were making their home debuts, and, of course, Manchester United would have to come from being behind!

United took the game to Charlton and created a number of chances that they could not convert. Yorke was looking right at home wearing the colours of his new club—it was as if it was his 100th game for the Red Devils at the 'Theatre of Dreams', not his first.

However, United were left frustrated just after the half-hour mark when Charlton took the lead against the run of play and in somewhat fortuitous circumstances. Mark Kinsella beat Schmeichel with a deflected drive to open the scoring. The Addicks manager, Alan Curbishley, stood on the touchline with a big smile on his face, and Charlton were in raptures, buoyed by an amazing play-off final victory a few months before when they beat Sunderland on penalties after the game had finished 4–4. Their first three games in the topflight since 1990 had seen them pick up five points from a possible nine, including a 5–0 victory over Southampton and a very creditable goalless draw away at Arsenal. Curbishley won the Manager of the Month award for August.

Given the form Charlton was in, fans were asking if Manchester United would fall victim to them now they had the lead. Or would the Addicks fall foul of the cursed Manager of the Month award?

With the on-going Sky takeover talks and United trailing in the game, the Old Trafford faithful could have been forgiven for being somewhat frustrated. That did not last long, though, and just seven minutes later, United were level. A good passing move between Yorke and Ole Gunnar Solskjaer resulted in the latter slotting the ball home. And then, on the stroke of half-time, Yorke headed the ball into the net, sending fans wild. Any nerves that the record signing of £12.6 million may have caused disappeared with that goal. Not one United fan would catch the wry smile made by Curbishley on seeing his team go one-up, but all saw Yorke's smile when the ball went into the net. It was very infectious, not only on the terraces but also with his new teammates. Henning Berg had seen the influence that the young Trinidad and Tobago player was having on the team even in his very early days. He would even make his manager and his captain smile, and that is exactly what was needed after the disappointment of the previous campaign, "We needed personality and a guy like Dwight Yorke to liven things up," said the Norwegian international, "Not to be too serious but have the right professionalism and work ethic at the same time. Everybody enjoyed themselves and we needed it at the time."

Yorke's second Manchester United goal came just three minutes after the restart. A Beckham delivery was touched on by Solskjaer, and Yorke was there to put the ball into the net. Yorke was smiling once again, and the vast majority of the 55,147 fans in the stands did so in unison. Ole Gunnar Solskjaer wrapped up the win for United in the 63rd minute when he headed in a cross from Berg. Yorke was beaming when he gave his post-match interviews, "This is what I dreamt of and I am looking forward to having more nights like this," he told the media. "I had nine fantastic years at Aston Villa, but this is why I came here. If someone had said to me before the start of the game that I would have scored, then I would have taken that, but to get two was superb. It's such a pleasure and a joy to play with such talented players. Everywhere I look there is just quality, whether it is Beckham on the right, Jesper on the left, or Keane in the middle."

Yorke's manager was also full of praise when he told journalists. "He was excellent. It's always nice to score on your home debut, and apart from that, his own contribution and ability to turn defenders gave us something extra." When asked about gaining their first win in the league and the team's overall performance, Ferguson replied, "It was a really good performance, and I could not have asked for better."

Charlton Athletic became the first club to endure a hiding from Manchester United in that season, but they would certainly not be the last. Two goals apiece from United's main strike force for the evening. A new partnership was forming, and as the fans poured out of Old Trafford, the excitement was palpable.

Was that the turning point and a reason for the supporters to keep smiling like Dwight Yorke?

CHAPTER SIX
A Whole New Ball Ache: The Story of the Proposed BSkyB Takeover

***

WATCHING LIVE FOOTBALL in the comfort of home surroundings was a rare experience in the 1970s and 1980s. Both ITV and the BBC would show the FA Cup final, but it wasn't just confined to the game itself. Both channels would broadcast the build-up for hours prior to the 3 pm kick-off. The European Cup final would also be shown, but not on both channels, and of course, we had the World Cup and European Championships. From 1983 onwards, both channels showed live games, but not every week, and it was regional, too, in some cases. Coupled with decreasing attendances at matches in the 1980s, mass unemployment, and the rise of the hooligan and football firms meant that going to the match was not deemed safe for families, even if it was affordable. Crumbling stadiums and poor facilities were also factors.

In 1989, Sky TV was launched. At the time of its launch, there were just four TV channels that could be viewed in Britain: BBC One, BBC Two, ITV, and Channel 4. In the early days of Sky TV, it offered four channels: The Sky Channel (now called Sky One), Sky Movies, Eurosport, and Sky News. It was the brainchild of the media magnate Rupert Murdoch, who had seen the benefits of cable channels in the United States.

Murdoch came to Britain in the 1960s and soon made his mark; he purchased the *News of The World, The Sun,* and *The Times,* as well as other media companies. Sky had been launched in a hurry to get ahead of its rival at the time—British Satellite

Broadcasting (BSB) which had the advantage of being backed by the UK's business and finance sectors.

Both companies were losing money in the early days as take-up was not as great as originally hoped, and they, therefore, merged in 1990 to become British Sky Broadcasting (BSkyB). Three things then happened that would catapult Sky into dreamland.

First, the beautiful game started to become beautiful once again. England reached the semi-final of the 1990 World Cup, held in Italy, and Paul Gascoigne became the most loved and recognised face in England. We also saw the romance of the Republic of Ireland as they reached the quarter-finals themselves under the guidance of one of England's World Cup winning heroes of 1966, Jack Charlton. Secondly, the ban on English clubs playing in Europe was lifted after a five-year hiatus. The ban was a result of the deaths of 39 Italian fans as trouble flared in the 1985 European Cup final, where Liverpool played Juventus at the Heysel Stadium, in Belgium. Aston Villa and Manchester United were the first teams back in Europe: Villa (UEFA Cup) as runners-up to Liverpool in the 1989–1990 season and United (Cup Winners' Cup) for winning the FA Cup. However, Liverpool were not allowed to enter European competitions for a few more seasons.

Then, at the close of the 1990–1991 season, a proposal was put forward to form a new league, one that would bring in greater financial rewards for the game. This new league would become independent of the Football Association and the Football League, allowing it to negotiate its own sponsorship and broadcasting rights. Now that English teams were back in Europe and winning trophies, all top-flight clubs put forward that the monies they would receive would enable them to consistently challenge Europe's elite once more.

On 27th May 1992, the FA Premier League was formed, and it was BSkyB that won the rights to broadcast live games for five years with a successful bid of £304 million. Football had changed forever, and with it, Sky and Murdoch became serious players. It became a success story, and no team would become more successful than Manchester United during those initial five years.

Proving just how successful the Premier League had become, when it was time to renew the next contract, Sky paid £607 million for its broadcasting rights. The gamble had paid off. Only this time, as well as owning the rights to broadcast games, Sky also wanted to own a club.

On 1st July 1998, Manchester United's chief executive, Martin Edwards, along with the club's lawyer, Maurice Watkins, had a business lunch with BskyB's chief executive, Mark Booth. Amongst the salient points to be discussed was the merits of potential pay-per-view options. What wasn't on the agenda, but known to BSkyB, was that Rupert Murdoch wanted to buy Manchester United Football Club. It would have made for a very interesting conversation piece when they got around to Any Other Business!

Whilst that may have come as a surprise to Edwards at the time, it would not be the first time that he had been involved in such talks. Martin Edwards had taken over from his father, Louis, upon his death in 1980. In 1984, he held discussions with Robert Maxwell, who was looking to table a bid of £10 million. Maxwell's bid was met with fan fury, and eventually, the deal was off. Five years later, Michael Knighton offered Edwards the same amount in a bid to buy Manchester United. Once more the deal fell through. A third potential takeover didn't come to fruition when United director Amir Al Midani was told the price was £30 million.

On the last day of May 1991, Manchester United became a public company when it floated on the London Stock Exchange. As United went on to become England's leading football team, investors started to see a healthy return on their shares.

The Irish Times reported on 9th September 1998 that "British Sky Broadcasting, the satellite operator in which Mr Rupert Murdoch's News Corporation has a 40% stake, will today announce a £625 million agreed deal to buy Manchester United Football Club. United's board has unanimously accepted the offer despite protests from politicians and fans. The price is higher than expected and was agreed after the board held out during 36 hours of meetings for a better deal. The takeover will have to be approved by the British Government, although BSkyB is confident that its purchase does not breach competition rules. On Monday, Mr. Peter Mandelson, Britain's Trade and Industry

Secretary, confirmed that the Office of Fair Trading would scrutinise any takeover before advising him whether it needed to be referred to the Monopolies and Mergers Commission."

It went on to add, "BSkyB owns exclusive rights to live Premier League football, and politicians are concerned that ownership of the league's top club would leave the broadcaster in an unhealthily dominant position within the sport. BSkyB is paying for the acquisition in an equal combination of cash and shares. United's management is expected to remain in place, but it is not known whether Mr. Martin Edwards, chief executive, will have a seat on the BSkyB board. The broadcaster is expected to defend the acquisition as a good deal for football and for the club. United is understood to have accepted BSkyB's arguments that being part of a larger group will allow it to compete more effectively. Following today's announcement, BSkyB will campaign to win round fans who have attacked the company's motives in bidding for the club. The company will seek to allay fears about big increases in ticket prices and the prospect of United's games only being available on a pay-per-view basis. It will stress continuity and say it has no desire to interfere with the club's day-to-day management."

From £10 million to £625 million in just 14 years! Not a bad increase! So, what was so compelling for BSkyB to make such a bid in the first place? Apart from the prestige of owning one of the biggest clubs in the world, BSkyB's contract at that time would take them to 2001. It was by far the largest TV company in the world, mainly due to its subscription base and associated advertising. The 1990s would be known as the 'real digital age' and with it came the opportunity for the big clubs to start looking at their own deals with TV companies. The viewing figures were blatantly showing that the likes of United, Liverpool, and Arsenal received far more public interest than the likes of Charlton Athletic and Bradford City. By inventing their own TV cartel, it would give the bigger clubs a much larger piece of the pie, either via its own subscription service or by pay-per-view. Specialist Football Fund manager, Tony Fraher, told *The Independent* in April 1999 that "it is now fairly clear that, when the current Sky deal runs out in 2001, every club will be negotiating its own deals for the rights to broadcast its home games." Fraher went on to add, "I reckon that 16 out of the 20 current Premiership clubs will be taken into media ownership within the next two years."

Murdoch and his team at BSkyB had seen the future of where football was going in the early 1990s and had secured the rights, not once but twice, and the figure that would be needed to be put on the table for the next one would be substantially higher. So, rather than being on the outside looking in, the plan was to be on the inside looking out. Manchester United were the hottest ticket in town and Murdoch wanted to sell those tickets to the highest bidder.

What is wanted in the boardroom is not necessarily what is wanted in the stands, though!

The backlash was immediate, and it was across the board. From supporters' groups to politicians—and even the FA itself. It also happened just before United's Annual General Meeting (AGM). Meetings of this type can be turgid affairs, but not this one. Over 1,000 fans packed into the Manchester Suite at Old Trafford, and voices were universal in their desire to pour scorn over the proposal. It was a torrid two and a half hours for Martin Edwards, with repeated requests for him to step down with immediate effect. Edwards would have expected this given the backlash prior to the AGM, but was left in doubt just how much this angered fans by the end of the meeting.

Graham Kelly was the FA chief executive at the time of the bid and said, "We have to assess the implications very closely indeed." A pattern was emerging with the concerns in that Rupert Murdoch would have a stranglehold on sport in the country, and this was just the beginning. Tony Banks, who was the Sports Minister at the time, stated, "This can't be treated as if it were just a normal takeover of one publicly quoted company by another." Banks suggested that the Office of Fair Trading (OFT) order an inquiry, and eventually, the OFT ruled against the takeover. The rationale was that it would be blocked as being uncompetitive. Following the ruling, Stephen Byers, Security of State for Trade and Industry, said, "Under almost all scenarios considered by the Monopolies & Mergers Commission (MMC), the merger would increase the market power, which BSkyB already has as a provider of sports premium channels."

Not everyone agreed, though.

Vic Wakeling, the Sky Sports MD, said, "We said at the outset that Manchester United had one vote in 20. We have then said, if people are concerned about this, we will agree to stand down during any TV contract talks, so we can't see why there would be a competition issue."

BSkyB chief executive, Mark Booth, was also very unhappy with the ruling, saying "This is a bad ruling for British football clubs, who will have to compete in Europe against clubs who are backed by successful media companies."

Despite Sky's protestations, most people agreed with the ruling, many of whom wrote letters and emails to the BBC to explain. Here is a selection of them.

"I fully agree with the government's action in blocking Murdoch's deal, which would have combined Britain's biggest pay-TV group and the world's richest soccer club. The BskyB's acquisition of Manchester United would have been against the public interest. A merger would have damaged the quality of British football by reinforcing the trend between richer clubs and poorer clubs. Consequently, it would have damaged first, British soccer and secondly, competition between broadcasters. The British government have strongly resisted against Murdoch's media empire, which includes four British national newspapers. There are good grounds for saying that the British government is going to ensure the 'independence' of soccer clubs. In this respect, a way should be found to develop together, sport and the media, because too much money is involved in British football."
Claire Marceau, France.

"The best news this year. Murdoch would have dragged UK football down and would have lost its inherent integrity and credibility. He must be shown that even though he sold his birthright (Australian) for money (US citizen), there are some things you just cannot buy. The UK's ethical values are higher than his, a lot higher."
George Cook, Australia.

"One needs to pose just one question, Why does Murdoch want to buy Manchester United? If the answer is "Murdoch is a rich fan

of Manchester United and football and just wants to indulge in a hobby, then there would probably have been no need to worry. But the real reason is to buy influence (for now or later) in support of his other media interests. This is not in itself sufficient ground to stop the sale if it could be said that Murdoch's and other media groups have/had brought any tangible recent benefits at all to the quality of television for viewers. That this has not happened is patently obvious to anyone with memories which go back longer than 10 years. The only beneficiaries have been shareholders in the media sector."
Malcolm Agnew, Germany.

"The government is totally correct on this point. I subscribe to Sky, and although they have an excellent sports coverage, they are trying to gain a monopoly in this. Make no mistake, it would only be a matter of time before they tried to take over more football clubs and starve the already hard done by public of the sport that we invented. Boxing has now been taken over completely, please can we make sure football and rugby do not totally go this way."
Carl Mustad, UK.

"A victory for football, genuine fans, and the (relative!) independence of a great, great club. Will go a long way to ensuring that the future of the game is not determined by the interests of broadcasters, who have little understanding of, or passion for, the game."
Lucy Burns, UK.

"Thank goodness, for once common sense prevailed. For once big business has lost out. It's very welcome. May this be the beginning of many more judgements against the Greed Factor."
Dave Waller, Canada.

"The correct decision. When I first read the article on BBC's website, I jumped out of my seat. I am very happy with this decision. Manchester United should exist as an individual company. The fans should own the team."
Zico, USA.

"I am so pleased that at last someone, somewhere, has given thought to the genuine football fan and seen that it was not going to be good for the game. I have supported United for 33 years and held a season ticket for 25 years, and when Sky said the silent majority were in favour of the takeover, that just wasn't true. It shows that they never bothered to find out what the average fan wanted, all they were interested in was making pots of money from us, they had no idea what the club means to us all. Anyway, I am really pleased, it's the best thing to happen at OT for a long time, now all we need is Martin Edwards to start listening to the fans."
Jackie Myerscough, UK.

"I think governments need to step in and protect the public by such trusts. It is a good decision indeed by the British government. What a change from the give-it-all-to-the-rich shameful era of Thatcher."
Aris, Canada.

"The government was right to turn the application down as it would have meant an even greater stranglehold on premiership football by one person."
David Banton, UK.

"What a magnificent decision by the DTI and MMC. Congratulations to Andy Walsh and all the boys at IMUSA. You mobilised the fans, organised a campaign on a shoestring, and played a significant part in ensuring that Murdoch would be defeated. BSB and MUFC spent millions of pounds to ensure that this deal went through, and to no avail. I could not be more delighted to see the share price fall on the strength of the announcement and hope that Martin Edwards will now do the honourable thing and resign from the Board. United are still playing for three trophies, but they have won the most important battle of the season so far; they have defeated BSB; the fans who campaigned against Murdoch should take a bow."
Carl Moynehan, UK.

"A good day for football. You only have to look at what the Murdoch empire has done to rugby to know that this was the right decision. If the bid had gone through, it would have paved the way for the media takeover of the top football clubs. Whilst a lot of cash would be generated, the gulf between the Premier and lower leagues would just get bigger. I don't want to see super clubs of expensive bought-in players and small exclusive super leagues—I'd rather sacrifice some international success and see some home-grown talent and some variety in the matches."
Andy Johnson, UK.

To tighten up procedures, to prevent this type of bid from occurring again, a ceiling of 10% ownership was introduced for any individuals or companies with shares in more than one club, and in November 1999, BSkyB was forced to sell 2.9 million of its United shares from an 11.1% to a 9.99% stake. So, in April 1999, the Government stopped the takeover of Manchester United Football Club. Football had won, and United fans were happy.

Not so much the board though!

The players were doing their talking on the pitch, and if the takeover had affected them, they certainly hadn't shown it. Quite the opposite, in fact.

CHAPTER SEVEN
Red or Dead—Game 8

"Will get up on the dance floor tonight."
Ed Sheeran, Foy Vance

***

Wednesday 16th September 1998
UEFA Champions League Group D

Manchester United 3 Barcelona 3
Old Trafford
Attendance: 53,601
Referee: Stefano Braschi, Italy

Manchester United: Schmeichel, Neville (G), Irwin, Keane, Berg, Stam, Beckham, Scholes, Solskjaer, Yorke, Giggs— Substitutes: May, Butt, Cole, Sheringham, Neville (P), Blomqvist, van der Gouw.

Barcelona: Hesp, Reiziger, Sergi, Barjuán, Enrique, Abelardo, Cocu, Figo, Zenden, Anderson, Giovanni, Rivaldo—Substitutes: Baia, Oscar, Ciric, Okunowo, Roger, Xavi.

***

MANCHESTER UNITED HAD passed the qualification test and made it into the group stages of the Champions League with relative ease. Their reward was a place in Group D alongside Barcelona, Bayern Munich, and Brondby. This was 'D', which must have stood for 'Death', as in 'Group Of Death'!

The first game pitted United at home to Barcelona. The last time these two giants had met was in 1994, in the group stages of the Champions League season. United had lost the away leg 4–0.

This time, at Old Trafford, in front of a crowd of 53,601, there would not be such a one-sided affair. Moreover, the total opposite. The game was filed under end-to-end and thriller.

United actually went into the match as favourites as the Catalan giants were missing several key players such as Pep Guardiola, Frank and Ronald de Boer, and Patrick Kluivert. It's not often that Manchester United have entered the 'Theatre of Dreams' playing in all white, but that is exactly what they did. It set the scene, which would become a common one during United's tenure in Group D—goals, goals, goals.

United took the lead in the 17th minute with Ryan Giggs heading home Beckham's cross from the right-hand side. The Red Devils were unlucky not to have gone in front just before Giggs's goal, when Solskjaer, again supplied by Beckham, had rattled the bar. United doubled their lead on 25 minutes, sending Old Trafford into raptures. A spectacular overhead kick from Dwight Yorke rebounded against Barcelona's keeper, Ruud Hesp, and evaded several players before being smashed home by Scholes. It could have been three when Solskjaer put the ball into the net, only to be judged offside.

Half-time came, and United were in dreamland, and revenge was on the cards. Barcelona had not read the script though and pulled a goal back in the 47th minute to slightly dampen the red spirit. Whether it was confusion in the defence or a lack of concentration so soon after the break, Anderson made it 2–1. Worse was to come on the hour mark when the referee, Stefano Braschi, awarded Barcelona a penalty after Stam was adjudged to have fouled Rivaldo. Giovanni stepped up and made the game all square. Just four minutes later, United restored their lead, this time courtesy of David Beckham, who, after a shaky start to the match, had really come into his own with a 25-yard free kick that sailed beautifully into the Barcelona net.

As befits games that are end-to-end, Barcelona came back and seven minutes later were awarded another penalty. A goalmouth scramble saw Nicky Butt handle the ball. The referee pointed to the spot and gave Butt a red card. Luis Enrique took the spot kick and made it 3–3. Alex Ferguson later described the ref as "a real shocker," but admitted United were overrun by Barcelona in the second half. A frustrated Ferguson said the decision to send off Butt was a bad one, but he also said: "We just lost impetus, and we lost our game plan and our shape. I'm quite happy with the result at the end of the day because we could have lost."

Ferguson was correct in that Barcelona did have one more chance to win the game when Anderson turned Roy Keane and lashed the ball just wide. Schmeichel remonstrated with his captain, complaining that he had been turned far too easily. The referee blew the final whistle, and those at Old Trafford and watching at home knew that they had witnessed one of those classic European nights when anything could happen. The United fans were not happy with the performance of the referee, though, and the chants of "The referee's a w*****" cascaded from the stands.

Whilst it is true that Barcelona were missing a few key players, they still had plenty of quality in the team. In his post-match assessment, Alex Ferguson told the waiting press that the game "had been the perfect football match" and continued, "both teams trying to win with scant regard for the consequences. That's how football should be played, and in a sense, this match was a throwback to the days before detailed organisation of teams."

It was one of those classic matches where no one team wins; football is the victor. It was a positive start to the campaign from both clubs. It was made even better by the news that Brondby had beaten Bayern Munich in their opening game, and hence, put both clubs above the German giants.

Those who thought that the return leg would be the complete opposite of what had occurred at Old Trafford were in for a surprise. United once more played in white when they battled Barcelona at the Camp Nou on Wednesday 25th November 1998. Both teams played out another classic with six goals shared. Anderson may have had a last-minute chance to win the game for Barcelona at Old Trafford in the first game, but it wouldn't take him long to get on the scoresheet, with an unstoppable shot in the first minute giving Barcelona the lead. Then, on 25 minutes,

Dwight Yorke equalised with a great goal of his own after some good work from Jesper Blomqvist. Yorke's strike partner, Andy Cole, then put United in front on 53 minutes before Rivaldo equalised just four minutes later. Yorke restored United's lead on 68 minutes when he headed home powerfully from a cross supplied by David Beckham. Not to be undone by Dwight Yorke was Rivaldo, who scored his second on the night with a clever overhead kick on the 73rd minute.

Clive Tyldesley was settling into his new role at ITV as the channel's main football commentator after taking over from Brian Moore. By Clive's own admission, he inherited a trusting relationship with Alex Ferguson and had become a welcome guest at the United manager's off-the-record ITV briefing before the big games. This did not mean that Tyldesley was immune to the hair dryer treatment, however, as it proved just before the return leg in Barcelona. The scene of the rollicking was in the foyer of the Grand Marina Hotel in the city. The young reporter had made his way to the lunchtime briefing with Ferguson and was sharing a taxi with Bob Wilson from the BBC. He was soon on his way back to his own hotel, though, with his tail and microphone firmly between his legs. Clive Tyldesley describes the scene: "A preview of the game had appeared in *The Sunday Times,* written by the press doyen that was Hugh McIlvanney. Hidden among the bard's flowing prose was a very strong hint that Wes Brown would be preferred to Phil Neville in order to combat the height and physique of Rivaldo on the Barcelona left flank. Hugh's long friendship with Alex Ferguson meant that there could only be one source for such speculation. Wes Brown's name was already on my team sheet. The evening before the game, I happened to step into the lift at our hotel at the same time as Neville Neville, the father of the famous footballing brothers. In a conversation lasting no more than a dozen floors, he confided that Phil was worried for his place in the team, and I tried to console him by saying that there could only be a change if the manager was worried about Rivaldo's height. No reflection on Phil's ability. Night, night, Nev."

Tyldesley continued, "Nev did not go straight to sleep that night. By the time I marched into the team hotel the following lunchtime, he had told his boys that Clive Tyldesley thought

Phil would be dropped. Er, not quite what I had said. Phil had told Gary, and Gary confronted the manager at breakfast about ITV knowing the line-up before the players did. I walked straight into a bloody ambush: "Who told you the team?" Alex Ferguson asked me menacingly before any pleasantries were exchanged. "I didn't know the team," I replied in all honesty. I can't recall the precise detail of the next line of the conversation. Or the next. Or the next. I only remember their seismic reading on the Richter Scale and that my part in the conversation was well and truly over. In a crowded hotel reception area, my character and fidelity were noisily being ripped apart by one of the most recognisable, and widely respectable, men in all of Europe. Fergie didn't lay a hand on me, but the ferocity of the verbal assault was such that I limped out of the hotel battered and bruised a few seconds later. My ears were ringing for days. I don't know who coined the phrase 'hair dryer' to describe one of the manager's infamous rebukes, but the blast of scalding, scolding hurricane air that came my way certainly made a few hairs stand up on end. Not so much a talking-to as a talking-at."

Two games and two draws against the might of Barcelona— that is what Manchester United's group qualifying games were all about in the 1998–1999 season. They would play one more game in the group stages, and it was a 1–1 draw with Bayern Munich. That meant that Bayern would go through as group leaders and United in second place, thus eliminating Barcelona and Brondby. United had gained some revenge against Barcelona for that 4–0 thrashing a few seasons before. They had passed the test in the group of death and come out of it with pride, integrity, and a whole bunch of entertaining games where goals became the order of the day.

Manchester United had played six games, winning two and drawing the others. No team had beaten them; they had scored 20 goals, conceded 11, and finished on 10 points. It had been swashbuckling, but Alex Ferguson knew that they would have to think more European and be somewhat more conservative as they entered the knockout stages. Ferguson knew this could be done and set out to make it happen.

Manchester United's mindset had been impeccable in the first half of the season. They had played the game and never the occasion. A winning mentality and never giving up on any cause was deep into the United psyche. Ferguson had a plethora of superb individual footballers at his disposal. They all knew that, but they also realised that the team was more important. That mindset would strengthen and go into overdrive in the second half of the season.

CHAPTER EIGHT
Red or Dead—Game 9

"Oh no, not again!"
David Bowie

***

Sunday 20th September 1998
FA Carling Premiership

Arsenal 3 Manchester United 0
Highbury
Attendance: 38,142
Referee: Graham Barber

Arsenal: Seaman, Dixon, Winterburn, Vieira, Keown, Adams, Parlour, Hughes, Anelka, Bergkamp, Overmars - Substitutes: Bould, Ljungberg, Wreh, Manninger, Garde.

Manchester United: Schmeichel, Neville (G), Irwin, Keane, Berg, Stam, Beckham, Butt, Blomqvist, Yorke, Giggs - Substitutes: Neville (P), Cruyff, van der Gouw, Scholes, Solskjaer

***

IF UNITED HAD raised the red flag gallantly and pushed it forward against Barcelona, they had positively changed it to white for their next game just four days later against Arsenal. They went into retreat at Highbury and succumbed to their second 3–0 defeat—their fourth loss on the trot—to their title rivals. Despite making two changes from the starting line-up from the game against Barcelona, it was a totally bad day at the office from the start. There is a well-known phrase that accompanies many a white-collar worker at the desk: *'some days one is a pigeon and some days one is Nelson's Column."*

Manchester United most definitely did not possess wings that day!

Arsenal totally dominated events and took a deserved lead after just 14 minutes when Tony Adams headed in from a Stephen Hughes free kick. The only real chance for United came when a 25-yard shot from David Beckham struck the post, went across the goal, and then outside the other post.

Arsenal really put their marker down for the home win a minute before the break when Anelka followed up his first shot after a save from Schmeichel to put the Gunners firmly on top. The theme continued in the second half with Arsenal in cruise control, and a third was added in the 80th minute when Freddie Ljungberg chipped Schmeichel with a consummate easing that typified the match. To make matters worse, Nicky Butt was red-carded prior to the third goal for a trip on Vieira as he was bearing down on goal—his second dismissal in consecutive matches. Nicky Butt needed to improve, and United needed to get back to winning ways, and quickly. It really was a game to forget for the Red Devils. At the start of it, the 2,000 travelling United faithful had been singing, "You're only one-season wonders." That turned out to be a faux pas and premature for the United fans, but such is the case when hindsight is a wonderful thing.

It wouldn't take much time before Arsenal took the lead and controlled the game, when their fans would respond in agreement and wrapped in total irony, "We're only one-season wonders," was the response.

The headline makers had come out with:

Ten-man United shot down by Gunners

After the match, Alex Ferguson was not in the mood to mince his words: "It's one I want to forget," concluded the United Manager. "Hopefully, this will not be repeated. When did you last see my team play as badly as this?"

Manchester United had played Arsenal twice in the space of a few weeks, and both times they had been beaten comprehensively. The United fans might have sung about the Gunners being the equivalent of one-hit wonders, but the reality was that it looked very much like their next single would also get to number one and become the year's best seller. The bookies were now making the North London team favourites to claim the title and possibly more.

Alex Ferguson posed the question about when the last time they had played as bad as they did at Highbury that day to the waiting media after the game. It was a question that, in all honesty, they could not answer straight away. It would be the last time that the United manager would pose such a question in the first place. United would play a further three times against their closest competitors during 1998–1999, and it would not get anywhere near as bad as it had done in the first two games. In fact, the complete opposite happened.

But for now, there were plenty of things that Ferguson and his players would need to ponder on. It could not happen again. Losing was one thing, but the manner of the defeat was unforgivable. They would have to put it right straight away and move on very quickly. Nothing less than a victory in the next game would do—any other result would not be accepted. The following few days of training would ensure Manchester United were prepared in the best possible way to ensure that outcome. And what better way to come back strongly after this defeat than a home game against Liverpool the following Thursday.

CHAPTER NINE
Red or Dead—Game 10

Bête Noire—A Manchester Meeting—Part 1

***

Thursday 24th September 1998
FA Carling Premiership

Manchester United 2 Liverpool 0
Old Trafford
Attendance: 55,181
Referee: Steve Lodge

Manchester United: Schmeichel, Neville (G), Irwin, Keane, Neville (P), Stam, Beckham, Scholes, Solskjaer, Yorke, Giggs— Substitutes: Butt, Cole, Blomqvist, van der Gouw, Berg.

Liverpool: Friedel, Berger, Bjørnebye, McAteer, Carragher, Babb, McManaman, Ince, Riedle, Owen, Redknapp— Substitutes: James, Leonhardsen, Fowler, Heggem, Matteo.

***

THERE ARE A NUMBER of concessions to be made when looking at what constitutes football's biggest rivalries. It can be for a number of reasons: political, religious, economic, social, geographical, and success. Sometimes it can be just one of these, or it can be a mixture. It can be a healthy respect, or it can be pure hatred. An example of healthy respect is Der Klassiker, where Bayern Munich lock horns with Borussia Dortmund, in Germany. Whilst there is animosity between the two sets of fans, it's generally the on-field activities that grab the headlines. This can be filed under success due to the amount of trophies both have won.

Contrast that with pure hatred and one does not need to look much further than games that feature Fenerbahçe against Galatasaray. Not only is there hatred, but this is very much a geographical one too. Whilst they are both Turkish teams, they actually play on two different continents. Galatasaray is situated on the European side of the Bosporus Strait, in Istanbul, whilst Fenerbahçe are on the Asian side. Murder, rioting, and fighting have been commonplace when these two giants of Turkish football meet.

There are many other examples that typify football's biggest rivalries. Most of these are locally based where bragging rights are dished out on the Monday morning, whether this be on the playground, in the office, or the factory. These are classed as local derbies.

The biggest rivalry in England is arguably played between Manchester United and Liverpool. This stems from two main reasons: economic and success. Up until 1893, Liverpool had prospered financially as it was the major seaport. Every ship or boat would have to go through it to do its business. Then in 1894, the Manchester Ship Canal was opened, a 36-mile canal that provided a direct route from the Irish Sea. Now the very same boats and ships could bypass the Port of Liverpool, and as a result, many locals lost their jobs and their incomes. This, understandably, caused resentment between the two major cities in the North-West of England.

The Manchester Ship Canal was opened on 1st January 1894, and on 28th April of the same year, Newton Heath (now Manchester United) played their first-ever game against Liverpool in a test match, with Liverpool winning 2–0—revenge for those people that were losing jobs. The dish best-served cold continued on 12th October 1895, when Liverpool ran out worthy winners by a score line of 7–1. Newton Heath gained their first-ever victory, 5–2, just a few weeks later on 2nd November. Both were Second Division games.

The game played on 24th September 1998, was the 180th meeting (in league and cup) of the giants of English football. Up until then, United had won 63 games, Liverpool had won 59 of them, and 57 games had ended up as a draw. Liverpool had won 34 major trophies, compared to Manchester United's 23. Liverpool ruled the footballing world from 1976 to 1990, and Manchester United had dominated ever since. Economic resentment from the past, mixed with being England's two most successful clubs, set this game apart from all others.

Having been mauled at Highbury the week before, the Liverpool game was going to go one of two ways for United. Lose or draw and it would have an adverse psychological effect on them, but win, and it would show the mental strength within Ferguson's team. There's a well-used phrase in football which goes something like, "It's not how you deal with your wins, moreover, it's how you deal with your losses."

Manchester United went on the offensive as soon as the Referee, Steve Lodge, blew his whistle to kick the game off. Alex Ferguson had added spice to the proceedings prior to the match as he labelled his former midfielder Paul Ince, who was making his return to Old Trafford for the first time as a Liverpool player, as a big-time Charlie. The media lapped it up and it was billed as a game that was Keane v Ince. The Irishman came out on top, just like the whole United team did on this Thursday evening. Solskjaer, Berg, and Scholes all came close for the home team before the breakthrough was made on the 19th minute, when United were awarded a penalty. Jason McAteer was penalised for a handball and Dennis Irwin stepped up and put the ball into the back of the Liverpool net. This prompted Liverpool to wake up a little, but even then, they were restricted to just one effort in the first half when a deflected shot from Ince was saved by Peter Schmeichel.

It had seemed for a while that United had decided to sit on their lead somewhat, and this started to frustrate the Old Trafford faithful as the second half commenced. Liverpool were enjoying a lot more possession as the game wore on, and it looked like they had equalised in the 63rd minute when Karl-Heinz Riedle put the ball into the net. However, Liverpool's joy was short-lived as the referee deemed the German offside.

Old Trafford was relieved, and now it was time for Manchester United to get back into first gear as this had been a warning to them. The game was effectively ended as a contest in the 80th minute when Andy Cole, who had come off the bench just a few minutes before, made an immediate impact, crossing the ball towards Dwight Yorke who helped it onto Paul Scholes, who dispatched the ball beautifully into the back of the Liverpool net to make it 2–0. The game ended with eight bookings, and with the United Fans singing, "Charlie, what's the score? Charlie, Charlie, what's the score?" Paul Ince replied with a two-fingered salute. It didn't matter, though, because United had won, and it meant that 63 wins for the Red Devils in this fixture, had now become 64.

Gary Neville was named Man of the Match. As a Manchester United supporter himself, he knew very well that the fans would not have accepted defeat so soon after losing to Arsenal. They had bounced back well, and even leapfrogged their opponents on the evening to go into third place in the Premier League. It really wasn't Liverpool's day at all!

CHAPTER TEN
Red or Dead—Game 11

"It was the first time that we met"
Freddie Mercury, Mike Moran

***

Wednesday 30th September 1998
UEFA Champions League Group D

Bayern Munich 2 Manchester United 2
Olympic Stadium, Munich
Attendance: 55,000
Referee: Marc Batta, France

Bayern Munich: Kahn, Babbel, Lizarazu, Jeremies, Linke, Salihamidžiⵥ, Jancker, Strunz, Élber, Matthäus, Effenberg—Substitutes: Kuffour, Scheuer, Fink, Tarnat, Daei, Göktan.

Manchester United: Schmeichel, Neville (G), Irwin, Keane, Neville (P), Stam, Beckham, Scholes, Yorke, Sheringham, Blomqvist—Substitutes: May, Cole, Cruyff, van der Gouw, Solskjaer, Berg, Brown.

***

IT REALLY WAS hard to believe that this was the first meeting in Europe between these two massive clubs. It would continue to provide United with a stern test and superior opposition in the supposed 'group of death' after their start against Barcelona.

There would not be a repeat of the six goals shared by both teams, but it did come very close.

It was a poignant return to the city of Munich for Manchester United. Their first visit since the Munich air disaster that occurred on 6th February 1958, which had claimed the lives of 23 people. The plane carrying United players and staff, as well as journalists, had stopped to refuel at Munich airport after beating Red Star Belgrade in a European Cup tie. Twice, the take-off had been aborted due to heavy snow, and the plane was able to get off the ground on the third attempt before tragically crashing.

So, it was a very emotional affair, and the minute's silence for the fallen was impeccably observed from all four stands. This may have been the maiden match between the clubs, but the people of Munich and Manchester had already got ties that would bind them forever.

Alex Ferguson had noted that his team would have to be at their very best at set pieces due to the size and power of the Bayern players and felt his best chances would be on the ground and in open play.

Bayern took the lead as early as the 11th minute, and it was a contentious goal scored by Giovane Élber, who looked suspiciously offside. The lead lasted for just 19 minutes. United had shrugged off the first goal, took the game to Bayern, and this paid off at the half-hour mark. The tussle between Bayern's French World Cup-winning left-back, Bixente Lizarazu, and United's English right-sided midfielder, David Beckham, had been a really fascinating one in the early exchanges of the match. Beckham got the better of his counterpart before crossing the ball and meeting the head of Dwight Yorke—it was a beautiful delivery, and United were back in the game. It also served as a milestone and a fitting way for United to get their 150th goal in European competition. The Busby Babes would have been proud of the way that the goal was engineered and executed by Beckham and Yorke.

Both teams went into the break on level terms, with United ahead on points, but it would not take long for United to gain the lead for the first time in the match. On the 49th minute, Paul Scholes picked up a pass from Dwight Yorke, but his touch was heavy and fortuitously bounced off Lothar Matthäus, leaving a 50/50 ball between Scholes and the Bayern and Germany international goalkeeper, Oliver Kahn, with the momentum on the Englishman's side, who courageously won the dual before walking the ball into an empty Bayern net.

United continued to take control of the game and didn't sit back, with Teddy Sheringham pulling all the strings in a deeper role than he was used to, but it was working with great effect. Sheringham was not the fastest of players, but he had an intelligent football brain and knew what positions to be in and where to play the ball to. It came as no surprise that he continued to play into his 40s in a glittering career for club and country.

Further chances came the way of United, with Sheringham, Roy Keane, and David Beckham all missing chances to put the game beyond the reach of their German hosts. Those missed chances spurred Bayern Munich back into action, with Peter Schmeichel having to be at his best to keep Bayern at bay. Now, time was ticking away, and it looked like United would inflict a second successive Group D loss on Bayern Munich and keep them bottom of the table. However, there was a last-minute twist. Bayern were awarded a throw-in, and they decided to ensure it went long into the heart of the United defence. Peter Schmeichel came out of his goal to punch the ball away, which was normally a routine action for the great Dane. This time, though, he completely missed the ball, and it dropped into the goal as Sheringham challenged Élber. Seconds later, the game was over, and four goals had been shared. Before the start of the match, United would have taken a draw, but they left Munich feeling that they should have actually won it. As was the norm for this United team and its manager, it was unified in its defence of Peter Schmeichel, who had made a costly mistake that, in all fairness, was totally uncharacteristic.

In his post-match talks, Ferguson told the media, "It was an error of judgment" and "It was a kick in the teeth, and Peter didn't deserve that."

Roy Keane was also backing his goalkeeper when he stated, "No player in the dressing room was blaming him for what happened."

The first two games in Group D had seen United pick up

two points. Crucially, they had not been beaten by the giants of Spanish and German football when many had expected that they would. They sat in third place, with Barcelona occupying top space after beating Brondby 2–0 at the Camp Nou. Despite the defeat, the Danish team sat in second place. The next two fixtures in this group would see United play Brondby home and away, and the same happening with Barcelona and Bayern Munich. United had put themselves into a great position and could have some confidence that progression into the knockout stages could be achieved. They had played two of the favourites and matched them both. In the case of Bayern, they perhaps should have come away with all three points, but the last-gasp goal scored by Bayern had stopped this from happening.

It wouldn't be the last time that drama would occur in stoppage time in a match between Manchester United and Bayern Munich during the campaign.

CHAPTER ELEVEN
The Events that Shaped the World in 1999

"Could have sworn it was Judgement Day?"
Prince

***

THE LAST YEAR of the decade, and the final year of the 20th Century, was dominated by two words—the millennium. Whether it was the Millennium Bug or the Millennium Dome, it was totally inescapable.

The TV channels were busy with their schedules, with all roads leading to 31st December 1999, especially the BBC with their ambitious special millennium extravaganza, *2000 Today*. The programme was hosted by a team of top names led by Gaby Roslin and Michael Parkinson. The BBC's £12 million coverage brought together broadcasters and some of the best-known faces on British TV to capture the dawn of the New Year across the world.

Veteran BBC journalist John Simpson reported on the first midnight from the Pacific island of Kiribati, while there was also live coverage as midnight chimed in a host of locations, including New York, Sydney, and, of course, London. Indeed, in London on 31st December, the Millennium Dome (now the O2 Arena) was officially opened for a very special event that was attended by a whole plethora of VIPs and dignitaries, including the Queen and the then Prime Minister, Tony Blair. Blair was high and generous in his praise for the way that the country celebrated this important passing: "What struck me both last night and again today is this real sense of confidence and optimism. You just want to bottle it and keep it."

Not everything was positive, though, leading up to the 21st Century. The world held its breath as the clocks turned to midnight in various time zones because it was all down to something called the Millennium Bug, also known as the Y2K Bug. It referred to potential computer errors that related to the formatting and storage of calendar data. A lot of computer programmes represented four digits with only the final two digits. This made the year 2000 indistinguishable from 1900, and it led to fears of catastrophic proportions that could bring down worldwide infrastructures over a number of different areas, such as the banking and airline industries. It caused panic leading up to the millennium, especially during 1999, and a lack of clarity caused concern and confusion to the public at large with many stockpiling food, water, generators, and even arms. The Government even produced booklets for every household with the imaginatively titled 'What everyone should know about the Millennium Bug'.

So, if the world held its breath on the stroke of midnight, it positively breathed out at 00:01, as very little actually changed—in fact, nothing changed, apart from the Century. It was mainly thanks to all the movers and shakers in the IT world that worked together to check, fix, and upgrade systems in readiness. Bill Clinton called it "the first challenge of the 21st Century successfully met."

It would not be the last!

Other things that happened around that time included:

Rogue trader Nick Leeson returned home to England from Singapore nearly four years after he was jailed there after his illegal dealings led to the collapse of Barings Bank with reported losses of £850 million.

TV presenter Jill Dando was killed on her doorstep at her home in Fulham.

1960s soul singer Dusty Springfield passed away after a battle with Cancer.

Construction began on the London Eye as it was lifted into position on London's South Bank.

Former Glam-Rocker, Gary Glitter, was jailed for four months at Bristol Crown Court for downloading child pornography. Glitter was caught after he had taken his computer into his local PC World to be fixed.

In the world of finance, the Royal Bank of Scotland launched a hostile takeover of NatWest Bank, and the Midland Bank changed its name to HSBC.

The biggest-selling single in the UK in 1999, went to Britney Spears when she scored her first number one with 'Baby One More Time'.

The biggest-selling album was *Come on Over* by Shania Twain.

The top movies of the year included: *Star Wars Episode 1: The Phantom Menace, The Sixth Sense, Toy Story 2, Notting Hill,* and *The Matrix*.

TV shows that made their debut in 1999 were *The Sopranos, Family Guy, The West Wing, Futurama,* and *SpongeBob SquarePants*.

It was also the year that Vladimir Putin became President of Russia after the resignation of Boris Yeltsin (7th May 2000)—and he's still in The Kremlin.

There were some notable sporting achievements outside of football in 1999. In Boxing, Lennox Lewis became the undisputed Heavyweight Champion of the world by defeating Evander Holyfield on the second attempt. Their first bout was a controversial draw.

The Fight of the Millennium occurred on 18th September, when Felix Trinidad defeated Oscar De La Hoya by a split 12-round decision to unify the IBF and WBC's world Welterweight Championship.

Golf witnessed both triumph and tragedy in 1999. The Ryder Cup was won by America after defeating Europe with the final score of 14.5 to 13.5, and Tiger Woods was named as the PGA Tour Player of the Year and also won the PGA Championship. Tragedy occurred when the American golfer, Payne Stewart, was killed in an air crash.

In Athletics, Michael Johnson set a new world record in the 400 metres with a time of 43.18.

Australia became Rugby World Champions by beating France 35–12 and became the first country to win the Webb

Ellis Trophy twice. Scotland were crowned the Five Nations Champions.

BillyJo won the last Grand National of the 20th Century at Aintree in Horse Racing.

The World Snooker Champion was Stephen Hendry, who defeated Mark Williams by 18–11, although John Higgins remained the Number One player for 1999.

At the end of January 1999, England Manager Glenn Hoddle was interviewed by Matt Dickinson of *The Times*. Hoddle was in no mood to pull any punches about how the media had treated him and his team in the aftermath of the 1998 World Cup. The relationships between the media and England managers have sometimes not been positive either regarding upcoming World Cup or European Championships tournaments. Indeed, the late great Sir Bobby Robson was called "Booby Robson" prior to Italia '90 and Graham Taylor was also on the receiving end after the failings in the European Championship in Sweden in 1992, when they called him and his team "Turnips." The vitriol against David Beckham had reached a fever pitch after France '98, and Hoddle was keen to go for the national media's throats. However, it was not the football aspect that grabbed the headlines. Moreover, it was his religious views, when he claimed that "people born with disabilities were being punished for the sins of a former life." Hoddle had expressed similar views in 1998 when he was on Brian Alexander's *Sports Week* show on Radio 5 Live. Hoddle said about his religious beliefs, "I have got an inner belief and an inner faith with God. I do believe spiritually we have to progress because we've been here before. The physical body is just an overcoat for your spirit. At death, you take the overcoat off, and your spirit will go on to another life in a spirit dimension. I think we make mistakes when we are down here, and our spirit has to come back and learn. That's why there is an injustice in the world. Why there's certain people born into the world with terrible physical problems, and why there's a family who has got everything right, physically, and mentally."

Those comments caused backlash and discussions everywhere, and in particular, in Parliament and with religious groups. Welfare groups described Hoddle as, "not fit to lead the national team," while Labour's first-ever Minister for the

Disabled, Lord Alf Morris, called his words, "grossly and unbelievably insensitive and hurtful."

Glenn Hoddle was quick to say that his views had been taken out of context. The England manager said, "I can assure you that is not what I said, and this is not what I mean." He went on to say that his comments had been, "turned on their head, misconstrued, misinterpreted."

Matt Dickinson, who had written the article for *The Times,* responded by saying, "I reported the interview faithfully and accurately, and now it's for others to draw their own opinions."

Glenn Hoddle's position as England manager soon became untenable, and he left the post just a few days later. Peter Taylor took over as interim manager for the forthcoming internationals before the position was permanently taken up by Kevin Keegan.

***

It would be so easy to just say that Manchester United won everything in 1999 and leave it at that. Of course, there was a lot more going on in the football world, therefore, I will leave out the achievements made in the Premier League, FA Cup, and the Champions League and discuss them in greater detail in forthcoming chapters. Well, that's what this book is all about, isn't it?

The only other domestic trophy, the League Cup, was won by Tottenham Hotspur by a single goal to nil against Leicester City. Allan Nielsen headed the winner in the final moments to give Spurs the victory.

In the First Division, Sunderland were crowned champions. It was a fantastic season for the Black Cats as they amassed a record 105 points, with Bradford City, under Paul Jewell's management, the surprise package as they finished as runners-up. They were joined in the Premier League by Watford who won at Wembley for the first time in their history when they beat Bolton Wanderers by 2–0.

At the other end of the table, Bristol City, Oxford United, and Bury were relegated.

Fulham won the Second Division at a canter, and like Sunderland in the First Division, did it with over 100 points, and Walsall came second.

Manchester City won the Second Division play-off final at Wembley by beating Gillingham on penalties after extra-time. They had been trailing by two goals with just minutes to go, but City pulled the tie level by scoring in the 90th and 95th minutes. York City, Macclesfield Town, Lincoln City, and Northampton were relegated from that division. It's hard to imagine Manchester City playing in a Second Division play-off final only 24 years ago, but that's football.

In the Third Division, Brentford made an immediate return as champions. Cambridge United secured the runners-up spot, with Cardiff City in third place, and Scunthorpe United winning the play-offs. Scarborough were relegated from the Football League, and Cheltenham Town were promoted in their place.

Perhaps the biggest story in the Third Division happened at Brunton Park, home of Carlisle United. On the last game of the season, they had to beat Plymouth Argyle to stay in the Football League. Carlisle had an injury crisis and they had secured the services of Jimmy Glass, a goalkeeper, on loan from Swindon Town because the league had sanctioned this outside of the transfer deadline. The score was 1–1 and deep into extra-time, seemingly with Carlisle dropping out of the league, they were awarded a corner. This was a now-or-never situation. Enter Jimmy Glass. He came up for the corner and duly slotted home to keep the club he had been loaned out to in the league. Lee Child couldn't have written a better script—a classic football moment if ever there was one.

The other European competitions were won by Lazio in the very final season of the European Cup Winners format when they defeated Mallorca 2–1 at Villa Park. Parma were crowned UEFA Cup Winners when they beat Marseille 3–0 in Moscow.

A lot happened both on and off the pitch in that year, but in terms of football, the story really belonged to Manchester United who ruled the sporting world in 1999.

CHAPTER TWELVE
Red or Dead—Game 36

Bête Noire—A Manchester Meeting—Part 2

***

FA Cup (Sponsored by AXA) Fourth Round
Sunday 24th January 1999

Manchester United 2 Liverpool 1
Old Trafford
Attendance: 54,591
Referee: Graham Poll

Manchester United: Schmeichel, Neville (G), Irwin, Keane, Berg, Stam, Beckham, Butt, Cole, Yorke, Giggs—Substitutes: Johnsen, Neville (P), van der Gouw, Scholes, Solskjaer

Liverpool: James, Heggem, Harkness, Carragher, Matteo, Bjornebye, Ince, Berger, Fowler, Owen, Redknapp—Substitutes: Kvarme, McAteer, McManaman, Leonhardsen, Friedel.

***

UNITED HAD TAKEN revenge on Middlesbrough in the third round of the FA Cup, winning the game by 3–1, just a few weeks after the Teesside club had come away from Old Trafford with the three points in the league.

Liverpool had overcome a tricky tie at Port Vale by winning the game 3–0. Now, the two giants of English football would face each other at Old Trafford for the second time in the season.

Liverpool could not breach the United defence in the league game but found themselves a goal up in the first few minutes of the FA Cup tie. This is how the BBC reported the visitors taking the lead: "With just two minutes on the clock, Patrick Berger and Jamie Redknapp linked up well in midfield, before sending Vegard Heggem clear on the right. The Norwegian wing-back clipped over a precise cross from the by-line, and Owen, unmarked on the six-yard line, sent a downward header into the bottom right-hand corner of Peter Schmeichel's goal for his 18th goal of the season."

Liverpool had shocked the home team, and it took a while for United to get into any kind of rhythm, although, they were very unfortunate not to level when Roy Keane sent a header goal bound. The ball hit the inside of the near post before deflecting off Paul Ince safely into the arms of David James.

The away team should have made it two shortly after when Robbie Fowler hit a speculative shot with his right foot that just sailed over the bar. The second half continued with United dominating possession, and Keane came very close to getting his team back on level terms on two separate occasions. The first was from a shot that deflected off Jamie Carragher and bounced just wide, and the second, a left-foot shot that pinged the base of the Liverpool goal.

Time was running out for United as the game entered its final 10 minutes, and it could have gotten worse for the home team when McAteer fed the ball through to Michael Owen, but his touch let him down and the chance went begging. Just a few minutes prior to this, Ferguson had rolled his last dice—super-sub, Ole Gunnar Solskjaer, coming on for Dennis Irwin. The other substitutes had been Paul Scholes on the 68th minute, replacing Nicky Butt, and Ronny Johnsen, replacing Henning Berg. Ferguson had to go for it. In the 88th minute, United were awarded a free kick, which was taken by David Beckham. His pinpoint cross was met by the head of Andy Cole, who placed the ball alongside the six-yard box for Dwight Yorke to tap home.

Old Trafford erupted, and the 8,000 travelling fans were shell-shocked, as were the players. Providing that United did not do anything silly, they had rescued themselves and kept their FA Cup campaign going.

The match was moving deeper and deeper into stoppage time, when Jaap Stam played a long ball forward that found its way to the feet of Paul Scholes. Was there going to be one last chance for him to put United through to the next round? That thought was inconceivable just a few minutes earlier. The fans jumped to their feet in anticipation. As Scholes prepared to shoot, Ole Gunnar Solskjaer nicked the ball, wrong-footed the Liverpool defence, and put it through the legs of Jamie Carragher and into the goal to seal victory for United. Progression was confirmed just seconds later when Graham Poll signalled the end of the game.

The away end was quiet; Liverpool were slumped on the ground, both supporters and players not really able to take in what had just happened—defeat snatched from the jaws of victory.

For Manchester United, it was the other way around, and bedlam began on the pitch and in the stands. They had made it 65 wins over their great rivals. Alex Ferguson, understandably relieved and happy at the same time, said, "Liverpool have every reason to be gutted. They defended fantastically but sheer determination got us through this."

It had not gone to plan as it had done in the league back in September—that had been pretty straightforward in the end. They had trailed for over 80 minutes, made substitutions that made impacts, and hit the opposition with two sucker punches that had finally floored the opponents at the death, and Ole Gunnar Solskjaer had been in the right place at the right time to land the final knockout punch.

United had made other comebacks throughout the season, but this was arguably the most significant one to date—and against Liverpool, it was so much sweeter for the Red Devils. The headline makers the following morning were using phrases like 'Smash and Grab'—which, of course, it exactly was. Their reward would be another match at Old Trafford in the FA Cup fifth round, and it would be stern opposition again, in the shape of Chelsea. They had come a long way since being thrashed by United in the 1994 final. It would not be an easy game for Alex

Ferguson and his team, but slowly and surely, momentum was on their side. Little did they know that they had already suffered their last defeat of the season, a loss to Middlesbrough in the Premier League in December 1998.

CHAPTER THIRTEEN
Red or Dead—Game 53

"You need hands to brush away the tears"
Max Bygraves

***

FA Cup semi-final replay
Wednesday 14th April 1999

Arsenal 1 Manchester United 2 (AET)
Villa Park
Attendance: 30,223
Referee: David Ellery

Arsenal: Seaman, Dixon, Winterburn, Vieira, Keown, Adams, Parlour, Ljungberg, Anelka, Bergkamp, Petit—Substitutes: Bould, Vivas, Overmars, Kanu.

Manchester United: Schmeichel, Neville (G), Neville (P), Keane, Johnsen, Stam, Beckham, Butt, Solskjaer, Sheringham, Blomqvist—Substitutes: Irwin, Giggs, van der Gouw, Scholes, Yorke.

***

THE FA CUP semi-final draw saw Manchester United take on Arsenal at Villa Park. It was a typical encounter between the Premier League's top two teams at the time. Arsenal started the match in a brighter fashion, but it was United who carved out the best chance in the early stages when Ryan Giggs shot over the bar after being put through by Andy Cole. Schmeichel was then forced into a save from a Tony Adams header, and he made another save from a fierce shot from Dennis Bergkamp. United had a goal disallowed when Roy Keane netted with a thunderous half-volley on the 17th minute; however, the celebrations were short-lived as Referee David Ellery judged United's skipper to be offside.

There were no goals scored in the 90 minutes, so the game went into extra-time.

Just four minutes into the extra-time, Nelson Vivas was given his marching orders for an elbow on Nicky Butt which allowed United to spend the rest of extra-time trying to take advantage of the extra man—but to no avail, as Arsenal's defence was resolute. The game ended goalless, and the replay was to be played at Villa Park once more, just three days later.

That game would arguably provide THE defining moment of the season for United.

The replay kicked off at 7:45 pm and the result wouldn't be decided until well after 10 pm. The drama and excitement was unremitting from start to the finish.

Somewhat surprisingly, Ferguson had decided that a number of his key players would start the game on the bench. The players left out were fresh, if and when required, and, given United were in the hunt for three trophies that season and had played 52 games already, United could ill-afford any injuries. He also had to ensure that his squad got as much game time as possible, so it was an astute move. Ferguson, along with his assistant, Steve McClaren, knew it would have to be a calculated balancing act. Dwight Yorke, Dennis Irwin, and Ryan Giggs would at least start the game as spectators on the bench, with Teddy Sheringham, Ole Gunnar Solskjaer, Phil Neville, and Jesper Blomqvist commencing battle upon hearing David Ellery's whistle at kick off time.

United drew first blood in the 17th minute, when David Beckham bent the ball past David Seaman from 20 yards after a smart lay off from Teddy Sheringham. You could say, no one bends it like Beckham, but it was a perfect execution from the right-sided midfielder. With the first goal in nearly 140 minutes of football scored by United, it gave them an extra spring in their step, and they had a succession of chances to double their lead. As the first half wore on, Arsenal came into the game more, and Schmeichel had to be at his best to deny Dennis Bergkamp and Emmanuel Petit. Manchester United went into the half-time break with a slender lead and they knew that they had to remain mentally and physically strong if they were going to keep it—they had the advantage, but the Gunners had the ascendancy.

United nearly doubled their lead after the break, but Ole Gunnar Solskjaer was thwarted by David Seaman in the Arsenal goal. Then in the 69th minute, the scores were level. Dennis Bergkamp did for Arsenal what Beckham had done for United in the first half, and from a similar range, although, the equaliser took a cruel deflection off Jaap Stam. It was of no interest to the Gunners because they were back in the game and that was all that mattered to them. Furthermore, Arsenal nearly took the lead just afterwards.

Roy Keane had a goal disallowed in the first game and it was now the turn of Nicolas Anelka to have a goal scrubbed out. Dennis Bergkamp had a shot saved and spilled by Schmeichel in the United goal and Anelka sneaked in, rounded United's 'keeper, and put the ball into the net. Everyone associated with Arsenal at Villa Park, at home or in the pubs and clubs, went delirious.

However, it was short lived though, because Referee, Ellery, disallowed the goal as Anelka was judged to be offside.

Parallels with the first game just three days before were plenty, and this continued with another sending off. This time it was Roy Keane who took an early bath for his second booking of the evening, a sliding challenge that took out Marc Overmars at full speed was enough for David Ellery to brandish a red card.

Now it would be Arsenal's turn to try and take advantage of the extra man and test United's mettle to the core. Then, deep into stoppage time and seemingly with the game going to extra-time for the second time in just three days, Arsenal were awarded a penalty after a rash tackle from Phil Neville on Ray Parlour. Arsenal celebrated. Convert this and the Gunners would be going to Wembley for the final.

In the United end, at both semi-finals, was United fan, Andy Synnuck. Born in 1964 in Altrincham. His early memories of

Old Trafford involved witnessing the genius of George Best, with his sports nut father. They would go many times together and formed a massive Red Devil bond. Andy's father passed away early in 1998 through cancer, so Andy decided that part of his grieving process would be to devote much of his time watching United home and away. It was to be his therapy and the grieving became a healing process.

Andy recalls the moment the Manchester United fans held their breath at Villa Park when Ellery pointed to the spot, "The guy next to me (who I didn't know from Adam) despondently took his car keys from his pocket. I defiantly slapped his thigh and growled at him, "he ain't effing scored it yet mate." Shocked, the guy sat down. I slapped his thigh again as Bergkamp struck the ball and it hit Big Pete's gloves. There was uproar in the stands. The man next to me put his keys back in his pocket and we smiled at each other. I apologised for the potential bruising on his thigh, although at that moment, I don't think he cared!"

On the pitch, the United players surrounded their goalkeeper, back slapping and hugging, and none more so than Phil Neville, whose relief was palpable. It was a massive let off for Neville and the Red Devils. What followed you just couldn't write a script for.

United were still in the game at that stage, and more importantly, were still on the hunt for that illusive treble, and as it turned out, it was that penalty save that would become the defining moment of the season. Peter Schmeichel, who had been derided by the media at the start of the season, would now become the hero, and they would be filling columns up with their accolades.

Arsenal looked shell-shocked as the referee blew the full-time whistle and extra-time beckoned. The Gunners tested Schmeichel in the early stages of extra-time, with that man Bergkamp trying to make amends for the penalty miss, but to no avail.

If the 93rd minute of the match would go into folklore history with that penalty save, then it was soon to be followed by the events that occurred in the 109th minute of that magical game at Villa Park.

Both sets of players had given their all over the two matches,

The pressure was mounting on Alex Ferguson during the 1989-1990 season.

Above: Mark Robins celebrates scoring arguably the most important goal of Ferguson's early tenure. It set United on the way to winning the FA Cup in 1990 (below).

The arrival of Eric Cantona in 1992 helped take United to the next level.

Steve Bruce and Bryan Robson lift the Premier League in 1993.
It was United's first title in 26 years. It certainly wasn't their last.

David Beckham's red card during the 1998 World Cup led to him receiving vicious abuse. Jimmy Greaves even suggested Beckham move abroad.

The first of United's 63 games of the 1998-1999 season ended in disaster - a 3-0 defeat to rivals Arsenal in the Charity Shield.

One down, two to go. United won the Premier League
on the final game of the 1998-1999 season.

The FA Cup followed six days later. A 2-0 victory over Newcastle United enough to
earn the Red Devils their second trophy of the season. But could they win all three?

Who put the ball in the German net? Ole Gunnar Solskjær.

History makers. The Champions League trophy completed a unique treble for Manchester United.

Every picture tells a story! From the fans.

THE F.A. CUP SPONSORED BY AXA · FINAL

MANCHESTER
UNITED
v
NEWCASTLE
UNITED

MANCHESTER UNITED

THE F.A. CUP

Wayne Rooney and Cristiano Ronaldo were the key players in the third great Manchester United team that Sir Alex Ferguson built.

The second time's a charm. In 2008 Manchester United won the Champions League for the second time under Ferguson's leadership.

but the difference was United were able to bring on some real big hitters as the match progressed, and Sir Alex's team selection had proved spot on—a masterstroke it could be said.

Enter one of those big hitters—Ryan Giggs. Intercepting Patrick Vieira's loose pass, Giggs strode into the middle of the pitch on the left-hand side, evading a tackle from Vieira who was desperately trying to make amends. In front of him stood the Arsenal rear-guard of Lee Dixon and Tony Adams. Giggs shimmied and strolled past them like they were invisible, before hitting the ball past David Seaman and high into the Arsenal goal. Now the delirium would be on Manchester United's side, and it would not be short lived either.

The image of Ryan Giggs with his hairy chest on display whilst waving his top in the air like it was spinning around in a washing machine must be one of the most endearing sporting images of all time.

Villa Park was rocking and there were no further goals—United won the game 2–1.

However, there was a price to pay for Giggs, as he left Villa Park on crutches, and he missed the next six matches. But he would be back before the end of the season.

Sir Alex was waxing lyrical about Giggs' wonder goal after the game, and he told the BBC, "Giggs' winner for me ranks with John Barnes' against Brazil for England, and Ricky Villa's for Spurs against Manchester City." He was also in awe of the goal that Beckham had scored but it seemed so long ago he probably couldn't have remembered it. Ferguson continued, "I have to say that within the context of this great game, the one from Giggs stands alone."

He was right of course.

Sports journalist, John Wragg, was working for *The Daily Express* in 1999 at the time, and he had a conversation with Sir Bobby Charlton after the game, "Bobby Charlton was almost shy about talking about it afterwards. One of football's great goal scorers had just seen Ryan Giggs score one of the best goals in football history. In the car park at Villa Park, as he headed back home, Sir Bobby stopped me and talked about what we had just seen. Bobby Charlton never courted publicity. He was happy with fame and recognition as a player, but late on that

Wednesday night of 14th April 1999 he talked with me about what we had just seen. Ryan Giggs had just sliced, turned, and sliced open again, an Arsenal defence meaner than the Chancellor of the Exchequer, to take Manchester United to the FA Cup final. It was a goal that beat their number one rivals at the time and had big consequences. Such ramifications from one goal in the 109th minute of a pulsating Cup semi-final replay. 'I don't want to say too much because it was the team who won that semi-final,' said Sir Bobby, 'But it was a wonderful goal wasn't it? Wonderful. That's Ryan Giggs. That's what he can do. When he's like that he's one of the best players in the world. I don't know if he can score one as good as that again, but I'd love to see it. I'm glad we've got him at United.'"

John Wragg continued his synopsis of the game, "People passed us in the late darkness of the night, some took a second take because it was Bobby Charlton, and then he left for the drive home with his wife Norma. Giggs hadn't even started the game, he came on for Jesper Blomqvist in the 61st minute. Beckham had put Manchester United ahead from long range in the 17th minute, Dennis Bergkamp did ditto for the equalizer after 69 minutes, and a Nicolas Anelka goal, following up a Bergkamp shot, was disallowed for offside. Bergkamp was the star of the show at that point, and I was working on my piece about his performance for *The Daily Express*. I was there, not to report the game, my colleague, Steve Curry, was in charge of that, but I was doing what we call a colour piece, words that describe the atmosphere, the light and shade of the game away from the blunt facts, and I was centring that around Bergkamp."

"Few newspaper readers realise that what they read in the morning with their toast has to be written during the heat of battle as it were, shaped as though it wasn't constructed as the game went on, but considered and reflected on in the calm after the final whistle. It's not easy. And it wasn't made easier when United, now down to 10 men with Roy Keane sent off, were a kick away from losing, as Phil Neville brought down Ray Parlour in the second minute of injury time. Bergkamp missed, Peter Schmeichel saved. Slight instant rewrite needed. Arsenal had the better of extra-time as I recall, and then Patrick Vieira gives the ball away. Shouldn't be a problem, though. It's in his own half and United have only got 10 men, but one of them is Giggs. It was just less than five minutes into the second period of extra-time.

10 minutes from the end. Vieira, unlike him as one of the giants of that Arsenal team, had been wayward with his passing most of the night. Arsenal were in the process of building an attack and were stopped and suddenly in reverse gear as Giggs got the ball. From beyond the halfway line, Giggs went past the recovering Vieira, and three of that formidable defence, Lee Dixon, Martin Keown, and Tony Adams. Arsenal had only conceded 17 goals in their 38 league games that season to finish second to United, so, add in Nigel Winterburn, and formidable is probably an understatement. Giggs slalomed on, Vieira probably praying for divine intervention as he watched Giggs hammer a shot over keeper David Seaman into the roof of his net. It was Giggs' 76th goal of his Manchester United career and we learned two things. One, when he whipped off his white Manchester United change kit shirt, that he's got a very hairy chest, and two, history was made. That will never happen again. Replays in FA Cup semi-finals were scrapped after that game. What a way to go."

Ryan Giggs would later concede that "this wasn't just a football match, but moreover a battle." If this truly was the case, then in sporting terms it was the Siege of Troy and of Stalingrad. It was Bosworth and it was Gettysburg.

For Ole Gunnar Solskjaer, it got him thinking that this was the start of something special for him, the team, and the fans. After 240 minutes of pulsating and gruelling football, United fans continued to drop words into conversations like "the treble" when discussing their team's chances of lifting silverware next month. They had booked their place in FA Cup final where they would face Newcastle United at Wembley. They had something new to put into their diaries, with travel and accommodation to book. London was calling once more.

For the United team, though, there would be plenty of work to do first and no one was getting carried away. The games were coming thick and fast and there was no time to dwell or indeed look too far into the future. Alex Ferguson wasn't going to get too carried away, that's for sure—he only ever takes one game at a time.

THREE GAMES IN MAY

The treble was clearly on, but first things first—Newcastle were officially now the team standing in their way of the first of three trophies on the horizon.

CHAPTER FOURTEEN
Red or Dead—Game 55

"It's Now or Never"
Wally Gold, Aaron Schroeder, Eduardo di Capua

***

Wednesday 21st April 1999
UEFA Champions League—Semi-final, Second leg

Juventus 2 Manchester United 3
Stadio Delle Alpi, Turin
Attendance: 60,806
Referee: Urs Meier, Switzerland

Juventus: Peruzzi, Ferrara, Birindelli, Pessotto, Juliano, Deschamps, Di Livio, Conte, Davids, Zidane—Substitutes: Montero, Foncesca, Amoruso, Tudor, Tacchinardi, Esnaider.

Manchester United: Schmeichel, Neville (G), Irwin, Keane, Johnsen, Stam, Beckham, Butt, Cole, Yorke—Substitutes: May, Sheringham, Neville (P), van der Gouw, Scholes, Solskjaer, Brown.

***

ITALY HAD PROVED to be a popular destination in the knockout stages of the Champions League for Manchester United. The quarter finals had seen them paired against Inter Milan with United taking the honours with a 3 - 1 on aggregate over the two legs. Dwight Yorke had scored two goals in the first leg at Old Trafford with no reply from the visitors, before drawing 1 - 1 in Milan. Nicola Ventola had given the Italian side the lead on 63 minutes, just a few minutes after coming off the bench as a substitute. United endured a sticky 25-minute period before Paul Scholes put the tie out of reach scoring in the 88th minute.

The semi-final would see Manchester United at home to Juventus in the first leg on Wednesday 7th April 1998. Juventus were vying for their fifth straight European final and moreover, if victory would be with the Old Lady, then it would see them into their fourth consecutive Champions League final. The bookies were in no doubt who the favourites were, and one only had to look at some of the players that manager, Carlo Ancelotti, had at his disposal. World Cup winners like Didier Deschamps and Zinedine Zidane alongside Edgar Davids and Filippo Inzaghi gracing the Old Trafford turf that evening. Alessandro Del Piero was not in the squad as he was injured.

United started the game brightly but it was the favourites who took the lead on the 25th minute with a beautifully executed goal scored by Antonio Conte. Edgar Davids had nutmegged Paul Scholes in the process after taking up possession from a typical midfield charge from Zidane. Juventus had dominated the first-half and the Red Devils were fortunate not to be more than one goal down at the break. In fact, it wasn't until the mid-point of the second half that United started to take the game to Juventus with Giggs and Keane testing the 'keeper, Peruzzi. Manchester United thought that they should have had a penalty for handball as Scholes shot wide from just 12 yards. United had the ball in the Juventus net on the 86th minute with a deft header from Teddy Sheringham who had replaced Dwight Yorke, but the referee deemed this to be offside.

However, just four minutes later they put the ball into the net and this time it was allowed. Juventus failed to deal with a cross by David Beckham and the ball found its way to Ryan Giggs who met it on the half-volley and smashed it into the net. Manchester United had been given a lifeline that in many ways that didn't deserve. An opinion shared by the *Daily Mail's* Graham Hunter. His article the following morning read, "Outplayed, outthought and utterly outperformed for 80 minutes, United were almost out of the competition." However, Alex Ferguson saw it differently and prophesised that something told him that his team would win in Turin and that Juventus may live to regret not taking their chances at Old Trafford.

The game was perfectly set up as Juventus and Manchester United took to the field for the return leg two weeks later.

United made three changes from the starting line up from the first leg with Henning Berg, Paul Scholes and Ryan Giggs making way for Ronny Johnsen, Nicky Butt and Jesper Blomqvist respectively. Juventus made just two changes with Ciro Ferrara, Alessandro Birindelli replacing Zoran Mirkovic and Paulo Montero.

Manchester United had been second best in the first leg so what the team needed to do was regain control and the best time to do this would be at the very start of the match to try and catch the Italian giants out. However, what the team did not need was to be a couple of goals down within the first 15 minutes and that was exactly where they found themselves. It left them desperately climbing a mountain – a mountain where it had rained for 40 days and 40 nights and where no real purchase could be found on foot as they slid backwards to the very bottom. Zinedine Zidane created both chances and Filippo Inzaghi inflicted the damage. Firstly, in the sixth minute, when the Italian marksman eluded Gary Neville at the far post to put the ball into the back of the net and then in the 11th minute when a shot from Inzaghi took a wicked deflection off the boot of Jaap Stam which sent the ball ballooning over the hapless Peter Schmeichel. United were shell-shocked and found themselves 2 - 0 down on the evening and 3 - 1 down on aggregate. Juventus were in dreamland and even though the game was in its infancy, the players could be forgiven to start to think about that fifth consecutive final appearance the following month. They would also need to heed the warning as it was Manchester United they were playing who had spent the whole campaign coming back from precarious positions and snatching victory from the jaws of defeat – and not in a lucky way either. They just did not know when to give in. It was by design and not default, but it would have to be THE biggest comeback of them all to make it happen.

In the 24th minute, United were awarded a corner from the right-hand-side. It needed a precision delivery and David Beckham swung the ball in and it was met by the head of his captain, Roy Keane. A beautiful deft header took the ball away from Peruzzi and his defence and into the back of the net. Keane did not celebrate as he ran back so Juventus could restart the game quickly. It was game on and Keane knew it – as did the rest of the team.

There's a saying that when a situation is tough and when the time comes, a man can turn the tide and win the situation. In other words, 'cometh the hour', cometh the man'. It sounds very much like a mythical or biblical quotation but it's neither and is commonly used in sport when the time is right to use it. The time was right in the 24th minute for Manchester United and shortly afterwards, a loose pass from Paul Scholes was picked up by the ever-dangerous Zidane. Keane went to make amends for his teammate but clipped the Frenchman and sent him crashing to the ground. The referee immediately brandished the yellow card. ITV was covering the game live in the UK, and its commentator for the evening, Clive Tyldesley straight away pointed out that meant Keane would miss the final due to the amount of cards he had received prior to this second leg. Keane knew it too. Lesser footballers may have let something like that impact their performance, but not Roy Keane. On the contrary, if anything it inspired him more. Keane had a tide to turn and nothing was going to prevent him from doing so. It was a masterful, determined, aggressive performance from him – there are not enough superlatives to describe Roy Keane's brilliant performance both physically and mentally in Turin at the Stadio delle Alpi in Turin that evening.

This is how Michael Walker reported the rest of the action for the *Guardian*, "At two down Keane initiated an inspirational resuscitation, rising like Tommy Smith 22 years previously for Liverpool in Rome to spear in a header from David Beckham's in-swinging corner. That was rousing in itself but 10 minutes later things got even better for United when Yorke hung in the air to steer in Cole's centre with his head with remarkable certainty. All was far from settled, though, and eight minutes after half-time Juventus looked about to book their passage to Spain as

Inzaghi bore down on Schmeichel, only to see his shot for a hat-trick rejected by a giant sprawl of a save. Almost at once Cole was let down by poor control at the other end, as Beckham's pinpoint cross found him alone in front of Peruzzi. Redemption was not far off. Ferguson, asked if this was the greatest night of his long career spanning Aberdeen and United, replied, 'I hope my greatest night is to come.'"

Alex Ferguson was in fine form also when he appeared in front of the ITV cameras to discuss the match, "It's a proud, proud moment for me. My players were absolutely fantastic, absolutely magnificent. I thought the first 45 minutes was the best in my time as a manager."

"You said this team would score, but to score three," continued *the interviewer.*

"Well, we gave them a start, didn't we?" said Ferguson. "But we recovered well, the players kept their composure, and I think they deserve to be there. It's a tragedy for [Keane and Scholes to miss the final], I don't know whether we can appeal or what, but it would be tragic for them to miss the final. I feel for them. It's a fantastic night for me. This is the level we want to play at."

Like his captain, Paul Scholes had been given a yellow card and would also miss the final, a final that would see them play against Bayern Munich for the third time in the campaign. Bayern had got through courtesy of a 1 - 0 home win against Dynamo Kiev and 4 - 3 on aggregate – exactly the same margin that Manchester United had got passed Juventus. Scholes had gone for a 50/50 ball in the 76th minute, with Didier Deschamps and the referee deemed that it was card worthy in the favour of the United midfielder. The Red Devils would be without two of their most influential in this key area on the park. There would be time to address this but United could soak it up that they had been a goal down in the first leg for much of the game and had come back from 2 – 0 down in Turin. The spirit in this team had not flown away.

The Treble was still on and United fans could dare to use these words in conversations still, as they had the previous week against Arsenal in their FA Cup semi-final. They could dare to dream still, but could they make it reality?

Just like the week before, Manchester United fan, Andy

Synnuck was there for yet another semi-final, "I travelled alone, although you're never alone with travelling Reds. Stadio delle Alpi, with all its history from Italia '90, hopefully not a bad omen for an English club. Outside the ground a member of the Carabinieri (Italian law enforcement) comes up to me (I had no colours on) and said, 'you English?' I replied, 'Yes,' and he said, 'Follow me' and he started herding up Reds. I was wondering what was going on and then a bottle smashed right in front of us, and then I knew why. I got in the ground OK, and there was a deafening atmosphere, with the beating drums, and Ultra's flags everywhere. I thought, well it's 14 years since Heysel and they know we hate Liverpool – not a bit of it. I remember a flag that boldly proclaimed, '**English We Remember You**' which wasn't a traditional welcome. What was it? 11 minutes in? Inzaghi had scored twice, and I thought "Holy shit that's it then." Unfolding on the pitch was arguably the greatest United performance I have ever seen. They got back into the game and started to dictate it (as much as you can against a talented Juventus team) and captain Keano rises to a corner and up we went in celebration. Despair turned to hope as the fans worked out and chatted that another goal and we're through, so we got another two for good measure! Yorke and Cole's interplay was a joy, and when the ball hit the net, deep joy. Final whistle Becks & G Nev and others came over to our section, yelling and screaming, kissing badges, all sorts. The torrent of missiles from the Juve fans up in the stands didn't bother us, we were through to our first European Cup final since '68. We were kept behind in the ground as a security measure, we were dancing to James 'Sit Down' on the P.A system. I left the ground with a lump in my throat, and close to a tear I do admit."

As the European campaign developed during the season, Peter Schmeichel described the focus as becoming more and more intense. David Beckham had stated that it was always the goal to be successful in Europe, and the manager had spoken about this a lot as a team and as individuals.

Now they were one game away from achieving this.

"Full steam ahead to Barcelona" was how Clive Tyldesley described it in the ITV commentary box.

Andy Cole described it simply, "Unbelievable, just

unbelievable. To win the game how we won the game – phenomenal."

It was becoming clearer and clearer how the season would now unfold.

Arsenal for the Premier League title, Newcastle United in the FA Cup final and Bayern Munich in the UEFA Champions League final were standing in their way in the three competitions they were still very much involved in as they would enter the month of May in 1999 – the month where winners are crowned!

CHAPTER FIFTEEN
Red or Dead—Game 61

"Helter Skelter"
John Lennon, Paul McCartney

***

Sunday 16th May 1999
FA Carling Premiership—Final Game of The Season

Manchester United 2 Tottenham Hotspur 1
Old Trafford
Attendance: 55,189
Referee: Graham Poll

Manchester United: Schmeichel, Neville (G), Irwin, May, Johnsen, Keane, Beckham, Scholes, Yorke, Sheringham, Giggs— Substitutes: Butt, Cole, Neville (P), van der Gouw, Solskjaer.

Tottenham Hotspur: Walker, Carr, Edinburgh, Freund, Scales, Campbell, Sherwood, Iversen, Anderton, Ferdinand, Ginola— Substitutes: Baardsen, Dominguez, Sinton, Clemence, Young.

***

THE FOOTBALL PURISTS will cite that the best finishes to a season, regardless of what league it is, are the ones that go down to the last game, or to use a well-coined phrase in football, go down to the wire. Whether it be the top-of-the-table clash with the winners being crowned champions, or a bottom-of-the-league battle with relegation on the line, seeing the 'as it stands' stats on TV (or nowadays on phones or tablets) provokes instant emotion. It is exciting but perhaps not so much for those teams involved.

Both Manchester United and Arsenal had gone into the last day of the league campaign on 16th May 1999, with a chance to be crowned Premier League Champions. Arsenal were vying to win it for the second season on the trot, and Manchester United were aiming to reclaim it. The stakes could not have been higher. United had the advantage of going into the game a point better off than their nearest rivals; they had on 76 points, whereas Arsenal had 75. The Red Devils also had a slight advantage in goal difference with a slender one goal in it. For Arsenal to reclaim the trophy they would simply have to win their game and hope that United lost theirs. A draw for the Gunners would be enough, providing Tottenham beat United by at least two clear goals.

Arsenal were at home to Aston Villa and Manchester United were at home to Tottenham Hotspur. The United game added more spice as they were playing Arsenal's local rivals in North London, but they weren't going to give in either—a win for the Tottenham faithful at Old Trafford was going to be bittersweet. A scenario going through their minds would have been that they could have come away with a famous last-day win, and providing that Arsenal saw the game through against Villa, they would have played a major part in helping their rivals win the league! That would have been the source of conversation pieces in North London all week leading up to this final day of the league campaign.

Whilst the Tottenham fans were stuck between a rock and a hard place, the players and the board would not have been. A victory and a Leicester loss or draw away at Nottingham Forest (who were already relegated) would have meant a top-10 finish for Spurs and led to greater financial rewards. They were going to provide a stern test for Manchester United regardless of the feelings of some of their fans.

Alex Ferguson had called the players in the day before the match. It was to be a light training session, nothing heavy, but just making sure that everyone was focused on what needed to happen the day after. The players were. The following day they were all at Old Trafford on time and sat down for their pre-match meal of pasta, and at 2:30 pm, the players gathered around for their team talk. All games were kicking off at the same time—4 pm—such is the (modern) tradition on the final day of the season.

Ferguson went through how he wanted the team to play and demonstrated this with his usual board, using magnets to show positional play. The players were already aware of their duties, but this was still an important process to follow, although, they had done it all season, so it was no day to make any changes. However, what the players were not aware of was who was actually playing until the team talk was over. The big talking point in the papers leading up to the match centred around whether Andy Cole would start the match, and, if not, then whom would it be? Teddy Sheringham or Ole Gunnar Solskjaer? The written press favoured Sheringham and called it correctly. Andy Cole was left disappointed upon hearing this straight from the horse's mouth, but he was on the bench and knew that he would give his all when the time came.

If Manchester United were to come out on top on that day, it would be Alex Ferguson's fifth league title, but it would be the first that they actually won on home soil. The Old Trafford faithful would make the 'Theatre of Dreams' a party place if the result went their way. The scene was set. The players with the ball. The fans putting both hands together, as if to offer prayer. The commentary pros with their mics, and the journalists with their pens and paper. This is how Stuart Mathieson from *The Manchester Evening News* reported on how the match went: "The team of the decade deservedly, and fittingly, will enter the 21st Century wearing the Premiership crown. Manchester United have dominated the 1990s, and it would have been a soccer travesty had Alex Ferguson's side been denied this conclusion to a sensational era in Old Trafford's history. Arsenal have been a dogged and resilient foe in this final, unbelievably-scripted campaign of the decade, and only those at Highbury and the blinkered anti-Manchester United neurotics could argue that there wasn't a more apt climax to the 1990s than a title victory at the 'Theatre of Dreams'. The Reds have blazed an unrivalled

80-goal scoring trail in the league for nine months, and have fended off the challenge of the Gunners, whilst storming to the Champions League and FA Cup finals on the back of a phenomenal 31-game unbeaten run."

"If there is someone out there who has been penning the text for this Premiership story then they really have drained every ounce of tension and have explored every conceivable ironic outcome to the chase. Never mind a whodunnit, this campaign has been a fanciful script for a 'who will do it.' And right up to the last minute, the potential for an incongruous ending was on the cards."

"The tone was set for a stirring finale by the rousing and dramatic voice of 26-year-old, Salford born, Red, Russell Watson, as the Opera singer boomed out Nessun Dorma before the kick-off. This was the song which heralded the decade back in Italia '90 and the translation of 'none shall sleep' was certainly apt. Nobody was going to dose off as this nerve-twitching last act unfolded. The stress was almost eased in the most bizarre fashion in the eighth minute when Dwight Yorke almost inadvertently scored his 30th, and most outlandish, one of the lot, when he charged down 'keeper Ian Walker's clearance, and the rebound agonisingly came back off the post. Having survived that embarrassment, Walker began to build up one of those performances you could feel may be talked of for years to come as the one which broke United's title challenge. Coupled with the Spurs' goalkeeper's defiant display, was a host of United chances which were being suicidally squandered. A flashing 18th-minute header from Ryan Giggs and an effort from Yorke which was dragged well wide increased the stress level. In a final week of the season, which was thrown up so many potentially ironic finishes, yet another presented itself in the 24th minute when Spurs silenced Old Trafford. Les Ferdinand was a Newcastle player four years ago when on the last day of the season, he scored against Spurs in a 1–1 draw, but it wasn't enough to halt United famously overhaul Kevin Keegan's one-time 15-point championship lead. Was Ferdinand finally going to have the last laugh on his 1996 tormentors and score a decisive last-match goal this time? It was an opportunist goal, that had the stakes not been so high, you could have admired. Walker launched a kick downfield and Iverson rose above David May to nod a ball into Ferdinand's path. Going away from goal, and policed tightly by Ronny Johnsen, the Spurs striker ran out of options and flipped the ball high over Peter Schmeichel. The Dane raced back in a valiant but vain effort to add to his club record of 178 clean sheets. But it wasn't to be."

"A ferocious hit from Paul Scholes in the 34th minute was parried by Walker, and the Reds midfielder followed up quickly, with a snapshot which the Spurs 'keeper again saved to add to the gnawing feeling that he was going to prove indestructible. Beckham raced to head over soon after the magnificent Roy Keane thundered past Sherwood, Campbell, and Edinburgh to set up Yorke, but his effort was blocked. Then, David May had the chance to equalise with a header from a corner which he sent sailing over the bar. It was an ominous collection of near misses, but United have made a habit of dramatic recoveries this season, and maybe it was always in the script that their famed resilience would be tested one last time in the Premiership."

"Old Trafford wouldn't allow the pace to ease off, and spurred on by a wall of sound, United finally made the breakthrough three minutes before half-time. The tenacious Scholes hunted down Sherwood and robbed the Spurs midfielder. Giggs took over, and then returned the ball to Scholes, who squared to Beckham. The big-game composure of his finishes never ceases to amaze. A shot swerving in from the angle he was at, I could understand, but Beckham amazingly curled the ball outwards in order to beat Walker and ended up sailing in at the far post. It was a sensational finish. United were in the ascendancy, and even the half-time break couldn't quell their revival. Andy Cole had kicked his heels on the bench for the first half, while Teddy Sheringham was given the opportunity to write his own personal, theatrical conclusion against his old club and the terrace taunters. Cole had his own ideas for an appropriately dramatic outcome. His first telling touch of the match was to expertly drag down a high ball from Gary Neville, then, audaciously flick it up again, and then, lob the advancing Walker. Scholes had a flying header whistle just wide and then Walker denied him again, and just as Iversen had a reply fumbled by Schmeichel, news came through that Kanu had put Arsenal ahead."

"Now a point would be no good to the Reds, and after Nicky Butt missed an 83rd-minute chance to put United in the clear, the minutes ticked slowly away until the final whistle at Highbury. Arsenal had won 1–0 and United had to preserve the lead. Spurs fans had urged Villa on earlier, and as their side launched a nail-biting last onslaught in injury time, you wondered if any Tottenham player had dared to level it up. It seemed like an eternity before Referee Graham Poll's final whistle was drowned out by an ear-busting roar, and Queen's 'We are the Champions' heralded scenes of delirious celebrations."

"Old Trafford hailed the team of the decade."

Meanwhile, Manchester United fan, Andy Synnuck, was making sure he was doing his late father proud by attending another game, "I drove to a mate's house in Radcliffe, Stoneclough, to leave the car. His wife drove us to Old Trafford, so we could enjoy a few pre-match beers. My ticket was in the Scoreboard End, behind the goal and just to the side. I had a great view. It was very much a carnival atmosphere with a few pre-match nerves, but it was certainly helped by the beer we had drunk! I can remember the eerie silence as Les Ferdinand's looping shot found the back of the net. On the TV replay, you could hear the 'plink' of big Schmeichel colliding with a post and falling into the side netting and popping out some of the plastic clips for the nets. Oh shit, this is not part of the plan, boys. United rallied, and Becks blazed a short-range header over the bar, which really should have been a sitter. Angry Becks! Then he got played in, in space just inside the box, and smashed it top corner, far side. It was 1–1. Cole came on as sub, virtually his first touch, an aerial ball came over his head, and his foot caressed the ball down and lobbed Ian Walker. Old Trafford just erupted. If there had have been an overall roof it would have come off! It was 2–1."

"Then the nail-biting commenced as the clock ran down to the final whistle of the League campaign. It was a very bizarre situation of Spurs fans willing us on to stop Arsenal winning the League! Then, relief, joy, as the ref blew his whistle, and we were the champions."

Andy Synnuck continued with his recollections: "My plans of collecting the car and driving back home ready for Monday work immediately went out the window as we searched for a celebratory beer. Coming out the of ground, Martin Tyler, the Sky commentator, rushed past us heading for his car, presumably. He gave us a wink and a smile, and said 'How was that for you lads?' Pretty damn good, Martin, cheers! When my mate's wife picked us up, we did a little cruise up and down Deansgate, with me hanging a large United Premier League champions flag out the back window! More beers back followed at my mate's house, and I stayed the night. I drove home for work at around 5 the following morning, in the wall-to-wall HGV scenery of the M6. I was tired but very happy. I guess I wasn't the only one at work that day."

Andy was not the only one!

Ged Duffy was at Old Trafford that day, basking in the glory of seeing his beloved Red Devils win the league on home turf for once. If Duffy had turned a different corner, he may well have been watching the match in his private box at the 'Theatre of Dreams'. Or, perhaps, he would have watched it from his Malibu home or New York penthouse. But he didn't. Ged Duffy is often cited as the unluckiest man in the Manchester music scene. He had the chance to manage *New Order* and he could have played bass for *The Cult*. His band, *Stockholm Monsters*, could have been the next big thing before *The Happy Mondays* and *The Stone Roses* broke through, as discussed once by the late great Tony Wilson. *The Monsters* also influenced *Oasis*.

Shoulda Woulda Coulda.

None of that actually happened, and that corner was not turned, but he was still a very happy man as Ged explains: "If United won then they would be champions, but if they drew or lost, and Arsenal won, then the title would go to Highbury. I was very confident as we were playing Spurs—we always beat them—and besides that, there would be no way their fans would be roaring them on against us as it would hand their biggest rivals, Arsenal, the title. The funny thing was that as the game kicked off it looked like Spurs were up for it. Les Ferdinand scored to make it 1–0, and the Spurs fans celebrated but quickly calmed down as the realisation sunk in about the result. United were throwing everything forward but the Spurs goalie was having a great day, and to be honest, the nerves were slowly creeping into the stadium. Just before half-time, the ball came to Beckham and Golden Balls just passed it into the net and the stadium erupted. The tension had been lifted and the noise grew. Andy Cole replaced Teddy Sheringham at half-time, and within two minutes, had scored a lovely goal to put us ahead. The Spurs fans were not really pushing their team, and they celebrated with us at the final whistle, and a few friendly North London chants were sang at their neighbours', Arsenal, expense. The players celebrated on the pitch with the trophy, and Fergie addressed us all with the message that the big one was in Barcelona. He wished us all luck in our travels to Wembley and Barcelona, and thanked us all for our great support."

One down, two to go.

CHAPTER SIXTEEN
Red or Dead—Game 62

"I am here for the goal, and the goal is to try to do it again"
Pete Sampras

***

Saturday 22nd May 1999
FA Cup (Sponsored by AXA)—Final

Manchester United 2 Newcastle United 0
Wembley Stadium
Attendance: 79,101
Referee: Peter Jones

Manchester United: Schmeichel, Neville (G), Neville (P), May, Johnsen, Keane, Beckham, Scholes, Cole, Solskjaer, Giggs—Substitutes: Stam, Sheringham, Blomqvist, van der Gouw, Yorke.

Newcastle United: Harper, Griffin, Charvet, Domi, Dabizas, Hamann, Lee, Solano, Shearer, Ketsbaia, Speed—Substitutes: Given, Barton, Maric, Glass, Ferguson.

***

THIS WAS TO be the second consecutive season that Newcastle United had reached the FA Cup final. They had been beaten 2–0 by Arsenal in May 1998. A goal from Marc Overmars and Nicolas Anelka in each half was enough to give Arsenal the double. The last time that the Magpies had won the FA Cup was in 1955. Now, they were back at Wembley again to see if they could win it for the first time in 44 years and stop yet another double from happening. This time it would be against the red of Manchester, not North London.

Manchester United had travelled down by coach, with the players fairly relaxed after the exhalations from the previous week when they had won the league. Whilst it may have been a relaxed atmosphere, the focus was still intact. One down and two more to go. United were still taking it one match at a time. Just like they had all season. They always played the match and never the occasion. It is what true champions do.

Andy Cole had been relegated to the subs' bench against Tottenham. Now, it would be his prolific strike partner who would do the same. Alex Ferguson had told Dwight Yorke that he would not start in the FA Cup final, citing the reason that he didn't want his record signing to pick up any knocks ahead of the Champions League final. Yorke was disappointed to be told this as he felt that Fergie should be picking his best team. Yorke could do nothing about the decision, and he had to be on top of his game, if and when he got the call. His inspiration for this would take him back to his buddy—Andy Cole. Cole had gone through the exact same issue before the Spurs game. He had come on and scored the winning goal to give United the championship. He had been Johnny on the Spot. Yorke's mentality would have to be the same. Whilst the disappointment was there, Dwight Yorke was a professional and a major part of this band of brothers. As it became apparent that United would be challenging on a number of major fronts, both Ferguson and his assistant, Steve McClaren, knew that the time to rest players and play the fringe 11 would have to be nothing short of perfect. It had worked so far, and it would have to work again. Newcastle United were about to find this out on a sweltering day in the capital.

The match report once again comes from Stuart Mathieson of *The Manchester Evening News*. Stuart had been covering Manchester United for several years, and the club had provided him with plenty of space to fill his columns. No more so than in May 1999. This is how he reported it. "Manchester United are the undisputed Kings of England and now for Europe. Immortality is beckoning the Super Reds and I expect that honour to be bestowed on them in Barcelona. United have a look of indestructibility about them. No matter what obstacle has been placed in their path this season, they've surmounted it. Whether the challenge was thrown down by opponents, fate, or self-inflicted, manager Alex Ferguson's incredible heroes have risen to the test."

"Wembley's poser never really looked likely to be set by Newcastle. And even United's infamous masochistic streak could never have contrived to have turned this picnic into a panic. So, it was the Gods who decreed that the Red's examination in the FA Cup final must be that they had to rip up their dressing room plan after two minutes and come to terms with the loss of inspirational Roy Keane. But for every victim, there is a victor, and the Irishman's misfortune was Teddy Sheringham's moment of glory as the much-abused Londoner imperiously steered United to the historic third double."

"In 1994 and 1996, it was the coolness of Cantona which clinched United their two previous domestic doubles at Wembley. In 1999, it was the steadiness of Sheringham that secured the climax to the two major domestic prizes. Sheringham has borne the taunts from the Capital about his lack of medals since he moved North in search of big-time silverware. Even in his hour of retribution a week ago, when he won the Premiership title in front of his Tottenham tormentors, Sheringham couldn't escape their wicked tongues. Within minutes of the striker being taken off at 1–1 and United going on to win 2–1 to lift the crown, the quick-witted songsters had formulated new words to their old ditty, and they sang: "Oh Teddy, Teddy they had to take you off to score the winning goal.""

"Well, Sheringham had been almost as rabid in confining that cruel jibe to the dustbin along with the original after just six days by coming on against Newcastle to ease United to a historic Wembley victory."

"Ruud Gullit has inherited a side with a reputation as the great cup final under-achievers. The Dutchman has discovered it is a dubious distinction that will take some shifting. The 118th FA Cup Final was the first between two Uniteds, but in truth, there was only ONE United at Wembley, and they were wearing red shirts."

"The Geordies came out all blood and thunder and seemed intent on discovering by muscle if United saw this as a sideshow before the big one in the Camp Nou on Wednesday. The victim of the early bruising battle for supremacy in the key midfield area was Keane, who, of course, won't even play in Spain along with his banned sidekick Paul Scholes. Gary Speed's crunching tackle on Keane in the second minute looked in the first instant a crude one. On second viewing, it was clearly nothing but a hard and fair challenge which had unfortunate consequences."

"It was all over for Keane, and with Nicky Butt, smartly attired in his Prada cup final suit, contemplating his job in Barcelona, the Geordie hopes rose as Keane and Sheringham crossed over on the touchline."

"Newcastle captain Alan Shearer must have wished he could have re-formed England's one-time formidable SAS international strike force in black and white stripes for the afternoon. On the ground where the pairing enjoyed many a glory moment, it was Sheringham who revived the best memories."

"Just 96 seconds after belatedly beginning his cup final, he had controlled a strong pass from Andy Cole which suspiciously looked like it was intended for Ryan Giggs. Whatever, Sheringham took the sting out of it, nipped between a couple of defenders, and played a pass to Scholes before cruising on into the box for the return and finishing it off with a crisp opener."

"Having fought through so many FA Cup epics, it seemed United had finally earned the right to a stroll. The Red's 10th-minute opener effectively ending the final as a contest, with Scholes and Beckham brilliantly ensuring there would be no foothold to be had back into the game in midfield, United were able to warm up for Barcelona in a manner that Fergie dared not had hoped for."

"Sheringham had two further chances in the first half to add to his tally, but one Beckham free kick brushed his hair in the 23rd minute, and a Gary Neville cross was powered just past the post in the 39th minute. Sandwiched in between was a glancing Ole Gunnar Solskjaer header, which probably should have been converted, and a Cole lob which would have been if it had carried a bit more space. The introduction of Duncan Ferguson at half-time provided Shearer a worthwhile partner and also gave the neutrals some hope of seeing a Wembley classic. United answered the 10-minute hint of a Geordie revival with a typical counterattack, which saw Giggs hunt down and hurry Dabizas into a weak clearance. Solskjaer nipped in to begin United's attack and play the ball into Sheringham. With his back to goal, he eased the ball into Scholes' path, and the Midfielder made up for his Champions League disappointment with the goal which clinched the double."

"Peter Schmeichel's final game in England saw him finish as he started with a clean sheet and his normal dominance was aided by the post, keeping Ketsbaia's drive out in the 57th minute, and substitute Silvio Maric fluffing a chance to set up a possible late comeback."

United fan, Ged Duffy, was at Wembley that day basking in the glory of a third double in just five years. He was grateful that the game had not been a bruising one given what was to come in just four days in Spain, as he explains: "We had driven down to Harrow, parked the car, and then got the train to Wembley. My wife, Lesley, and her mum had come down with us and they stayed on the train and went shopping in central London. I would never normally do that before a cup final as I would be nervous and not want family distractions pre-match. It was a weird atmosphere for a final as we knew that we would win, and we did so at a stroll, with no danger caused by Newcastle at all. Roy Keane went off injured after only seven minutes and normally when Keane, who was the heartbeat of the team, wasn't there we would not be as confident as usual. Fergie must have felt the same as us as he didn't replace him with another midfielder. No, he put Teddy Sheringham on, and it was like Fergie was saying to all of us, 'don't worry, this will be a stroll in the park.'"

"Within 96 seconds of coming on, Teddy passed the ball into the net. The game was over. Just after half-time, Paul Scholes scored to put the game to bed. I have never felt as relaxed at a game as I was that afternoon, Newcastle was never going to bother us. Afterwards, the celebrations were muted as if everyone was saving themselves for the big one on Wednesday in Barcelona, even though we'd just completed our third league and cup double in five seasons, which is mad when you think about it. I remember walking back to the train station and Newcastle fans were screaming at United fans to celebrate. It was a very strange situation. They were all singing and shouting, and if you didn't know, you would think that they had won it. Two down, One to go. Full speed Barcelona."

Ged Duffy's first game watching United had been on 13th April 1974, when they had, ironically, beaten Newcastle 1–0. A couple of weeks later he was back at Old Trafford to see Dennis Law back-heel the ball into the net, to give Manchester City a 1–0 victory and put another nail into United's relegation coffin. Law did not celebrate and just left the pitch with the game not actually finished, with fans on the pitch and fights breaking out between red and blue. The scoreline did stand though. Now, he was going back to Manchester from Wembley with a few quid in his pocket, with clothes to pack, and dreams in his head to win another trophy at the Camp Nou in just four days' time. No player was walking off the pitch and games would conclude.

Just how Game 63 would conclude, nobody could have predicted.

CHAPTER SEVENTEEN
Red or Dead—Game 63

"Great is the art of beginning, but greater the art is of ending"
Henry Wadsworth Longfellow

***

Wednesday 26th May 1999
UEFA Champions League—Final

Bayern Munich 1 Manchester United 2
Camp Nou, Barcelona
Attendance: 91,000
Referee: Pierluiga Collina, Italy

Bayern Munich: Karn, Babbel, Tarnat, Kuffour, Linke, Jeremies, Basler, Zickler, Jancker, Matthäus, Effenberg—Substitutes: Helmer, Scholl, Strunz, Fink, Salihamidzic, Dreher, Daie.

Manchester United: Schmeichel, Neviile (G), Irwin, Blomqvist, Johnsen, Stam, Beckham, Butt, Cole, Yorke, Giggs—Substitutes: May, Sheringham, Neville (P), van der Gouw, Solskjaer, Brown, Greening.

***

MANCHESTER UNITED FANS had left Wembley on 9th August 1998, to the sounds of the followers of Arsenal gloating and singing songs about how they were now the number-one club in the land after the Charity Shield. This was shared further afield on the TV, radio, and in the newspapers. Had the sun set on United? It had been a fantastic eight-year period for Fergie and the club, and perhaps there really was a wind of change blowing towards North London.

Now, on 26th May 1999, Manchester United were playing their final game of a gruelling campaign that had seen Storm Alex knock the wind of change that was heading down the M1 back up the M6. They had reclaimed the league and the FA Cup in the previous two games. The third time in the 1990s that Manchester United had won the double.

But this was different—very different, in fact!

Another game and another victory would mean another trophy—and the treble!

Standing in their way was Bayern Munich. Up until the 1960s, domestic German football had been largely amateur, and indeed, the Bundesliga did not come into formation until 1963—and that was just for teams that played on the West side of the Berlin Wall. It wasn't until the reunification of Germany that teams from the East were allowed to play, in the 1991–1992 season.

Bayern Munich had been crowned Bundesliga Champions for the first time in 1969 and had gone on to win it 13 more times, also winning the German cup nine times. They had also become a force in Europe, and by 1999, they had won all three major trophies—the European Cup Winners' Cup in 1967 and the UEFA Cup in 1996. However, it was the European Cup where Bayern had made the football world sit up and take note. Winning the competition in the 1973–1974 season against Atlético Madrid, they would go onto successfully defend their title by beating Leeds United in 1975 and St. Etienne in 1976—they were the third team to have won it in three consecutive seasons or more. The others had been Real Madrid and Ajax. Ajax had completed this remarkable task in the previous three campaigns before Bayern; Real Madrid had done it five times from 1956 to 1960. In total, Bayern had reached the European Cup final on two other occasions, when they were runners-up to Aston Villa in 1982 and Porto in 1987.

This was to be Bayern's sixth appearance in the final, and it was United's second.

This would be the third time that the teams had met in Europe, following the two group stage games earlier in the season. Those fixtures had ended in draws, but the third game would offer no such outcome. There had to be a winner, and the bookies had made Bayern Munich the favourites to lift the trophy.

Barcelona's Camp Nou was the perfect stadium to host the final. It was the largest stadium in Europe and could seat 99,345 people at its capacity. It was the second time it had hosted Europe's most prestigious competition, the first being in 1989. It had been expanded in 1980 in preparation for the World Cup in Spain in 1982. It was even used for the 1992 Summer Olympics.

Manchester United would wear their traditional red shirt, and Bayern reverted to their third kit to avoid any clashes as both teams wore red with pride normally.

As always with a team under Alex Ferguson, preparation was key. After the FA Cup final victory, he had moved the players to Bisham Abbey in Marlow, England's training complex at the time, before they moved to St George's Park. There were to be no heavy party after securing their third double—light training and practising penalties was the order of the day. On the Sunday evening, the players watched a video of the two games they had played against Bayern Munich in the group stages. Discussions focussed on what they had done well, what they needed to retain, and what they could improve.

The next day, the players and staff boarded Concorde, and this is where the real preparation began. The importance of having a good and secure hotel was key to Alex Ferguson, and they found this in the sleepy seaside resort of Sitges, a town just 25 miles south-west of Barcelona. The surroundings were perfect for the players to find some kind of relaxation, or as much as they could do at the least, and it worked a treat. Andy Cole likened the situation to trying to relax in a hotel before a third-round cup tie against teams from lower leagues, A few United fans had been in and around the hotel, and whilst this didn't overly bother Alex Ferguson, he did make it very clear that they were not to bother his team's preparations, and the fans duly obliged. Who could turn down such a direct request from the gaffer? Alex Ferguson would later offer an apology to the fans for just how direct he had been with them. Although, one suspects that those fans would have taken on board exactly what they had been told and the apology was not needed.

It certainly wasn't for Chris Morley, who had managed to get some photographs with the players with his sons, Simon, Graeme, and Robert. The family had travelled over with a group from their family home in Davyhulme in Greater Manchester for the final. "One of the guys in our group knew the kitman, Albert Morgan, but we could not get to him. The reason for this was that all the players and staff were around the poolside, and security were not letting non–residents into the hotel. It was manic, so we asked Paul Scholes to go and get him for us. In typical Scholes style, he told us to get him ourselves! Anyway, we managed to get some photos of the players. These were: Ole, Becks, and Keano. The other thing I remember about that day was Fergie giving Wes Brown and Jonathan Greening a right rollocking for sunbathing. He told him that it was draining them. My sons, Graeme and Robert, had managed to sneak poolside and overheard this. We thought it was a good idea to leave them alone after that."

Alex Ferguson and Steve McClaren's process of thought pertaining to team talks was to keep it as simple and as direct as they could be. These would take into consideration three key areas: the United team selection, Bayern Munich's tactics, and the third covered set pieces. Each component was vital, but just how telling the third would be would really come to the fore at the Camp Nou on the night.

The night before the match, the United players didn't get much sleep. Andy Cole had been one of the first to admit this at the breakfast table the following morning, and others followed. A mixture of excitement, nerves, and trepidation had been the main reasons as to why the Sandman had not entered like he should have had.

The match was to kick off at 8:45 pm local time, and the time delay could have had a detrimental effect on the management and the players. As is customary in Spain, the players took a siesta after lunch. Ole Gunnar Solskjaer was sharing his room with Jaap Stam, and the big Dutchman's snoring kept the Norwegian awake. Ole tried to watch a film but couldn't concentrate, so he called up his friends in Norway and he informed one of them that he felt like he was going to do something big in the game.

The journey by coach to the stadium began, and the relaxation had been understandably replaced by nerves. The time was now, and it started to hit home. The journey was one of quietness and reflection.

Once the players had arrived at the stadium, it all became real. The atmosphere in the dressing room was still reflective, but Ferguson had made sure that focus was paramount. He informed his players that they had already faced their toughest opponent—Arsenal. Rather prophetically, he also made a point that if Bayern were to score early, they would shut up shop and that his players would need to be prepared.

In only the fifth minute of the match, Bayern were awarded a free-kick just outside the United penalty area when Carsten Jancker was judged to have been felled by Ronny Johnsen. Mario Basler took the free-kick, bent it low to evade United's wall and Peter Schmeichel, and went straight into the back of the net. It was such a bad goal to give away, as Andy Cole explains in his autobiography, "We had jumped in the wall and the ball went the other side." It was exactly the start that United didn't want, but the saving grace was that it was only the fifth minute, so there was plenty of time to put it right—and they had experienced plenty of comebacks during the past nine months. None more so than what they had done in Turin just a few weeks before the final. They just needed to pull the rabbit out of the hat one more time. Alex Ferguson had already warned them that this could happen, and they would have to react in the way that he wanted. All season, fight had overcome flight for the Red Devils, and now they would have to do it one more time.

But would this be a touch too much for United?

Andy Cole had the first real chance to level on the 15th minute when he got himself into a dangerous position in the Bayern box, but could only watch the ball fly harmlessly past Oliver Khan. Schmeichel had to get down just two minutes later to prevent Zickler from putting Bayern two goals to the good, but real goalscoring chances were few and far between with Bayern Munich playing a close game, preventing United from getting into their stride as the half-time whistle was blown.

The second half also saw chances at a premium, with the

pattern of play not straying from the first period. There is no middle ground when it comes to cup finals—they are either exciting or drab affairs, with this one firmly falling into the latter. Manchester United were frustrated, and Bayern were frustrating. But it was advantage to the team from Germany, and that is all that mattered as the game wore on.

Then, in the 67th minute, United were awarded a corner. Before Beckham could take it, Sir Alex took Jesper Blomqvist off and replaced him with Teddy Sheringham. The corner came to nothing, but the attacking substitution signalled that the Red Devils would be going for it in the last 23 minutes, plus stoppage time. It was to be Bayern Munich, though, who looked more likely to extend their lead when they hit the post after good play between Scholl and Effenburg in the 72nd minute with a shot that was at least 30 yards out when he struck the ball. A minute later, the same player tried to lob the ball over Schmeichel; however, the great Dane managed to get a hand to it and turned it around the post for a corner. Just six minutes later, the Germans once again spurned a great chance to wrap up the match when they hit the bar. A surging run by Mario Basler saw him go past David Beckham before finding Scholl. This time the chip evaded the hands of Schmeichel, who was relieved to see the ball rebound to safety. United could not believe their luck, and it once again came their way in the 83rd minute when Jancker hit the bar following a corner taken by Basler in another pivotal moment. Another chance not taken by the Germans. Two minutes earlier, United had taken off Andy Cole and replaced him with Ole Gunnar Solskjaer, and it was almost an instant impact as the young Norwegian had a header saved from Oliver Khan. United could sense blood, and Bayern had missed some serious chances to put the game to bed. Time was running out for Manchester United, and it seemed like an eternity ago when Basler had given the lead to Bayern in the sixth minute.

Then in the 87th minute, Teddy Sheringham had a great chance to equalise when his shot was superbly saved by Khan, after a great back heel from Solskjaer. Yorke was next to find himself in a dangerous position, but he fell over the ball.

Bayern tried to take the sting out of the game by making a last-minute substitution. It looked increasingly likely that Basler's goal was enough to give the glory to Bayern as he left the field to wild applause from the Munich faithful to be replaced by Hasan Salihamidžic. The 90 minutes were up, and Bayern were still leading 1–0, a lead that had lasted for 84 minutes. The board signalled just three minutes of injury time. United had made so many significant comebacks in the dying minutes of games all season; now they were required to do so one more time. It had come down to those moments in football and sport in general—the now or never ones. Three minutes, and a goal to take the match into extra-time was what United now desired. The only thing they had on their minds was a goal.

During injury time, UEFA officials were already pinning the Bayern Munich ribbons onto the most prestigious of European trophies, but as the ribbons were being attached, Manchester United were awarded a corner. With nothing to lose, they threw everything but the kitchen sink forward, including the towering sight of Peter Schmeichel, who made his presence known in the opposition's area. David Beckham floated the ball into the box. It evaded heads and bodies—although according to Dwight Yorke, the ball did skim the top of Schmeichel's head—before it ended up on the far side of the penalty area, where Ryan Giggs met the ball on the volley. It was a crisp drive, but it was going wide until Teddy Sheringham turned it goal-bound and into the back of the Bayern net. The scoreboard flashed up the score:

Bayern Munich 1 Manchester United 1

Enter commentary folklore. Clive Tyldesley had become ITV's main football commentator after the retirement of the excellent Brian Moore following the 1998 World Cup Final between France and Brazil. Tyldesley was in the commentary box alongside the punditry of Ron Atkinson and said, "Peter Schmeichel is forward. Beckham. In towards Schmeichel. It's come for Dwight Yorke. Cleared. Giggs with the shot. SHERINGHAM!"

It was pure drama, and total elation followed from the players on the pitch and on the bench, in the stadium, and all over the world. United HAD done it once more. They had taken the game into extra-time, and they could regroup under the guidance of Ferguson when Italian referee Pierluigi Collina would signal the end of the 90 minutes.

However, there was still time for United to win another corner just before the final whistle blew, and again, it was taken by Beckham. This time though, Schmeichel would not make the same journey as he had done a minute before—he wasn't required to because United had fought their way back into contention. No silly mistakes. See this corner out, and then it's extra-time and the distinct possibility of that 90s favourite, the golden goal. Beckham once more floated the ball into the box. However, this time it didn't evade any heads as Teddy Sheringham met it to move the ball closer towards the Bayern goal. Before the Bayern defence could react, Ole Gunnar Solskjaer stuck his foot out, taking the ball high into the goal. Enter commentary folklore number two from Clive Tyldesley: "Is this their moment? Beckham, into Sheringham. AND SOLSKJAER HAS WON IT!"

Manchester United had saved their greatest comeback, in a season of great comebacks, to the very last game. The elation experienced just a minute earlier went into overdrive. Not only had United clawed their way back into the game, but they had also actually taken the lead, almost in the blink of an eye.

Bayern were shell-shocked, and soon after they kicked off, Pierluigi Collina blew his whistle to signal the end of the match. The final score beamed from the screens in the stadium and in homes, pubs, and clubs all over the world.

Bayern Munich 1 Manchester United 2

What drama had just taken place! At the time, there was no pause for reflection, but those three minutes personified what one goes through, not just in football but in sport in general.

"We are going to lose the game and it's dejection.
It's the hope that kills us!
We have drew level.
And the hope is sparing our lives!
We have taken the lead, and it's rapture!
We have won the match, and it's euphoria!
Push aside those that whisper never!
Always believe!"

In his post-match report for *The Manchester Evening News*, Stuart Mathieson made his opening gambit, which was to the point: "Manchester United, Champions of Europe. Doesn't it just look and sound good!"

Mathieson continued, "The incomparable history-making Reds have written a fantasy finish to their glorious treble success that was beyond belief, even by their outrageously dramatic standards. Where do you begin with the plaudits for such a phenomenal side and such an exceptional achievement? Barcelona '99 will go down in the Old Trafford annals as the most astonishing chapter ever in the history of the club. Wembley '68 won't be forgotten. That was the groundbreaker and it was a courageous and emotional triumph for Sir Matt Busby's European Cup winners. But for sheer drama, the Camp Nou theatrics will forever be imprinted on the memory. I said it after the epic Arsenal FA Cup replay, and I'll say it again. Keep all your memorabilia because you are going to want to say—I was there!"

This extraordinary night in Barcelona also produced some of the most memorable quotes from the players, management, UEFA officials, commentators, and the media. Alex Ferguson as usual had the vast majority of them, as you'd expect, saying, "This is the greatest moment of my life, and I'm struggling to take it all in. I haven't said anything to my players yet. I've just hugged and kissed them. I've slobbered all over them."

Others include:

"I was just starting to adjust to losing the game. I had reminded myself to keep my dignity and accept that it wasn't going to be our year. What then happened simply stunned me."
Alex Ferguson.

"It would have been Sir Matt Busby's 90th birthday today, but I think he was up there doing a lot of kicking."
Alex Ferguson.

"I told them the cup is only six feet away from you at the end of this day. If you lose, you can't even touch it."
Alex Ferguson on his half-time team talk.

"When I saw Basler waving to the fans, it gave me the hump: I wanted to get out there and show them."
Teddy Sheringham.

"When Teddy scored, I thought yes! I'm going to play 40 minutes of a Champions League Final. That's going to be unbelievable."
Ole Gunnar Solskjaer.

"We had to score some goals after the pressure we had. It's unbelievable, and it's very difficult to describe how I feel just now. But if people still wonder why I stayed at United, they can see why. The team spirit, it is unbelievable. Everyone works together and is in this together."
Ole Gunnar Solskjaer.

"This has been a marvellous season. It's been marvellous for the fans—the FA Cup, the Champions League, and in our own championship, and the players have been just great. I'm really proud of them. English football has been in the wilderness for a long time, and now we're back on the world stage."
Sir Bobby Charlton.

"It could take days, even weeks, to recover from such a blow. Losing in such a way is very tragic. It is inconceivable what has happened tonight."
Ottmar Hitzfeld, Bayern's Head Coach.

"They could not have won it like a normal team. Not these men. Not these remarkable, unstoppable, unbeatable men of Manchester."
Martin Samuel, *Daily Express*.

"In two astonishing, almost surreal, minutes at the end of the last European Cup final of the 20th Century, the gilded youth of the most famous of clubs left excellence behind them and found the greatness they have been searching for."
Oliver Holt, *The Times*.

"We have new superlatives now when the conversation turns to *extraordinary deeds in sport. We can recall the courage of Ali, the cold-eyed winning instinct of Lester Piggott, and Ian Botham's innings at Headingly. But always, we will come back to the night United beat Bayern Munich at the Camp Nou. It wasn't a comeback—it swept beyond the limitations of that term. It was a resurrection.*

They won so dramatically that the history of this wondrous competition has a new and permanent asterisk against the line which records United's 2–1 triumph. It must say, "Won in extraordinary circumstances—possibly divine."
James Lawton, *The Daily Express.*

"Even if you only saw it on TV, you don't much like football, and can't even stand Manchester United, it was a two-minute miracle you will tell your grandchildren about. The final 120 seconds of the 1999 European Cup Final in Barcelona were simply the most breath-taking in sporting history. The two minutes transcended sport. It was an object lesson in life. What those late goal scorers, Sheringham and Solskjaer and 11 other players achieved in those moments inspired me. Because of those two minutes, I will always know that if you keep trying, you can succeed."
Jonathan Margolis, *The Daily Mail.*

"Yet again in the crucial game, the English team has proven inferior to the German team. Maybe I shouldn't say it, but I promise never to say it ever again. Football, as Gary Lineker once said, is a simple game; 22 men chase a ball for 90 minutes, and at the end, the Germans win."
Marcel Reif, German TV Commentator.

"I'm sorry."
Lennart Johansson, UEFA President to Sir Bobby Charlton, when passing him to make his way down to the pitch after 90 minutes.

"When I saw Peter Schmeichel running up the pitch for the corner, I knew it was almost over."
Nicky Butt, Manchester United midfielder.

"Can you fucking believe him!?"
Alex Ferguson, to his assistant Steve McClaren on seeing Schmeichel going up for the first stoppage time.

"Sheringham! Name on the trophy."
Clive Tyldesley, English TV commentator, after 90 minutes 36 seconds.

"Hang on a second. Something's happening out there..."
Alex Ferguson, before the second corner is taken, in reply to assistant Steve McClaren's suggestion that they revert to 4–4–2.

"Is this their moment?"
Clive Tyldesley, English TV commentator, after 92 minutes 5 seconds.

"And Solskjaer has won it! Manchester United have reached the promised land!"
Clive Tyldesley, English TV commentator, after 92 minutes 17 seconds.

"Are you crazy?
Gerhard Aigner, UEFA General Secretary, inside the stadium, having just finished putting Bayern's ribbons on the trophy when an aide rushes in to tell him to put Manchester United's colours on.

"The lift took a half-minute to arrive, then you had to go through a long hall, through several rooms, and through the dressing room area, and because we were inside, we never heard a thing. I then saw out onto the pitch, and I was confused. I thought, it cannot be, the winners are crying and the losers are dancing."
Lennart Johansson, UEFA President, post-match.

"I can't believe it. I can't believe it. Football. Bloody hell."
Alex Ferguson.

The quotes attributable above have weaved their way into football folklore. One particular favourite is the one made by

ITV's Clive Tyldesley as the game entered its final stages with Bayern Munich seemingly with both hands on the famous trophy: "Can Manchester United score? They always score!"

Clive Tyldesley recalls the last 10 minutes of the final and his feelings of how Hocus-Pocus football can be at times—especially in the cauldron of THE hottest of games, "And so it is that when a team is leading 1–0 entering the final 10 minutes of a Champions League final and then hits the opposition woodwork a couple of times, an air of dread sets in. Oh no, one of those nights, and by the same bewitching formula, the team that is on the verge of losing takes mystifying heart from the fact that their hopes are hanging by an ever-thinner thread."

Football has given us many such moments. There is no logic to it, and perhaps this is the real beauty of the game? It allows for contrasting emotions, sometimes all at once, and this is universally accepted. Maybe it is magic!

Clive Tyldesley continued, "Bayern Munich teams are traditionally hewn from black forest oak and founded on rock mined in the Bavarian Alps. They don't crumble or choke. For what seemed like centuries, hardened winners like Oliver Khan, Steffen Effenberg, and Lothar Matthäus have been taking medals out of English palms like the proverbial sweets from a baby. This looked like a lost cause. Matthäus even went off to wash his hands ready for the trophy lift. But then Scholl's chip hit a post, then Solskjaer came off the bench, then Jancker's overhead kick struck the bar. Then, then, then. One after another, a chain of events unlike any we have seen all night. A charm bracelet being linked together before our very eyes. Even Bayern began to wonder. Every spin of the wheel was landing on red. Every roll of the dice was a United flush. For the first time all evening, they looked like scoring."

"Can Manchester United score, they always score."

"My words before the first of the two corners that landed the great sting were more proverb than truth. They were factually incorrect. United had drawn 0–0 at Blackburn just a fortnight earlier in a critical league game. They didn't always score. It just seemed like it."

"Driving to Wembley for the FA Cup final the previous weekend, I'd heard Mark Lawrenson offering a prediction on BBC Radio Five: 'Well, it won't be United nil, will it?' he said when asked for a score line. Maybe that was the phrase that infiltrated my increasingly desperate ramblings as the clock ticked beyond 90."

"There was momentum and there was previous. In the FA Cup semi-final, Giggs scored his giant slalom of a goal against Arsenal when it was decisive. In Turin, Keane headed his captain's goal when it was needed. In the title decider, Beckham struck his pure equaliser after Spurs had gone ahead. The stars just kept on aligning. One more constellation goal required."

Tyldesley went on, "The commentary position at Camp Nou is not far from the moon. It feels like the viewing gallery on top of a skyscraper. There are three rows of sharply tiered tight-fit seats and narrow desks, a sloping ceiling, and a partially glassed front divided by grills. Sitting on the back row, you look down at the distant field through a kind of letterbox. You can see the pitch, but you can't really see the stadium. I wouldn't necessarily have chosen that particular perch for the most important three minutes of my career. But choice had left the giant building. Kismet had taken its seat."

"Lennart Johansson, the UEFA president, was summoned from his seat in the VIP area to take the lift down to pitch-side in order to present the trophy. Bayern President Franz Beckenbauer accompanied him. When the elevator doors parted at ground level, they were informed that United had equalised. When the doors opened up again back up at the VIP level, they were informed that United had won. Neither of them witnessed either goal. Thankfully, I saw them both."

"There were exactly 102 seconds between the two goals. My best work was done during the first eight of those seconds. I said nothing at all. My best words all night followed that eight seconds of thinking time. 'Name on the trophy.' The great engraver-in-the-sky had long since gone to work on the European Cup. Teddy Sheringham's swept finish was only the equaliser, but Bayern were beaten. They knew as surely as a boxer stopped in his tracks by a stunning straight jab, that the knockout blow was on the way soon. It had been in transit for several months.

The BBC's long-standing Boxing commentator, Reg Gutteridge, had been a major inspiration to the young Tyldesley when he set out on his mic-to-mouth journey. "I'd like to tell you that I heard Reg's voice echoing around my head during those eight seconds." Tyldesley continued, "All of those breakfast-time phone reviews, all of his golden nuggets, 'What was the story, Clive?' 'Did you tell it during your commentary?'

"The big red circle around United's date with destiny appeared to have been drawn long before they touched down in Barcelona. That was the story. Their name, their time. It wasn't the whole truth of it. I'm not having that. I don't do horoscopes and Gypsy Rose Lee. It wasn't luck any more than (Johan) Cruyff's gnarled gum landing on the evening dew brought him luck. This was one of the superstitions that the Dutch master would go through before every match he played in."

"The winning goal was fashioned by the best ball striker in Europe finding the head of the best near post header in Europe finding the foot of the best poacher in Europe. Talent wins football matches, but fate's finger often seems to point them in the direction of victory."

"'Football, bloody hell.' The greatest post-match television interview ever given. Alex Ferguson's admission that he had no idea how his team had won. Reg didn't call me for a couple of days after that final. He gave himself some of his beloved thinking time. When his critique arrived, it came with as much pride as praise. I had learnt well."

"A few of the things I said in the eye of the cyclone have flatteringly become part of the screenplay to the night: 'Manchester United have reached the promised land,' and 'everything their hearts desired.' If the big moment arrives on your watch, it deserves more than amazing, fantastic, incredible, unbelievable.

"It's actually happened, so capture and establish the moment. Make it yours. Goals do belong to commentators. I was paid to re-record some of the audio accompanying United goals for the class of '92, and the producer asked me to put a voice on David Beckham's long-range missile against Wimbledon at Selhurst Park. I refused."

'No, that's Motty's goal,' I protested.

'It doesn't matter, does it?' came the irritated reply.

Yes, it does matter. It certainly matters to football fans, to whom the goal matters. John Motson's BBC commentary is part of the memory of it. A goal that will be talked about and replayed for years. Motty is the soundtrack to that goal like (John) Travolta is to the soundtrack to Grease. Anybody else is karaoke. The most recited words I uttered in Camp Nou broke the cardinal rule of commentary: 'And Solskjaer has won it,' committed the eternal sin of waving the winner across the line before the line had been crossed. If Bayern had somehow equalised and gone on to win a penalty shootout— and they could have! There'd be an effigy of me hanging from the entrance to the Arndale Centre by midnight. It would have been my fault."

The national newspapers were also waxing lyrical and had created some really powerful headlines that found themselves on the front pages as well as the traditional back ones:

The Express headline:

UNITED

The Times headline:

THE DREAM COMES TRUE FOR UNITED

The Independent headline:

UNITED WIN TREBLE WITH MIRACLE DOUBLE

The Daily Mail headline:

THE HEROES WHO UNITED THE NATION

The double winners had become treble winners in a matter of days, making history in the process. Winning the Champions League also meant that United became the first team to ever win the competition in its current format after not winning a major honour the season before, either domestically or abroad.

Manchester United were now in a group of exactly ONE.

There were scenes a plenty that followed the winning goal from Ole Gunnar Solskjaer. The players that had come up for that last corner were all there in close proximity. Stunned that they had firstly just got back in the game and now just seconds later they had taken the lead. Not really taking it in but moving closer together, hugging, embracing—all as one.

The same was true on the terraces, in the pubs and clubs, and at home. Not just with friends and family, but by kissing and hugging strangers. The first player that went over to Fergie was Ryan Giggs. They had been through so much with each other since the early days of the 1990s. It was a fitting meeting in the moment for the Master and his Protégé and showed just how far they had both come in the journey that took Manchester United to become kings of Europe.

And then there was Peter Schmeichel's celebration. He had not gone up for the second corner and would have been protecting the comeback with his mind firmly on the impending extra-time and possible penalties scenario. Now that was all forgotten as he celebrated on his own in his penalty area by doing cartwheels, something mainly reserved for children, not grown professional sportsmen. But it didn't matter—it absolutely did not.

So, a third trophy in May was lifted. This time it would be held aloft proudly by Peter Schmeichel, who deputised as captain for the suspended Roy Keane. A fitting way to bow out after eight glorious years as United's number one. A guard of honour was made by the team for Keane and Paul Scholes, who was also suspended. It was a thoughtful gesture by the team, but Paul Scholes would later claim that it had embarrassed him.

Roy Keane was more forthcoming in his view that the medal meant little to him. In a video that crops up from time to time on social media, Keane said, "I didn't play, did I? I don't know why people don't understand when I answer. They say, 'well, you got the medal,' but I didn't play." Keane then went on to state, "How can that be the same? It's not the same; I wasn't even a sub. I wasn't in the squad; I was in the stand with a shirt and tie on. I think it took 13 games to get to the final, and I played in all of them, but I missed the big one. I got a medal; they gave me a medal, but it doesn't mean anything to me. I remember going back to the dressing room and joining in, but, deep down, you are thinking you don't want to be there. It's one of the most natural feelings in the world; you're just on the edge looking in, and it's very hard."

That was the only negative on what had been a brilliant and

historic night for Manchester United. Keane and Scholes should have been in the United red shirts but wore the official grey suit instead. Both reportedly got bladdered after the game, and who could honestly blame them? Alex Ferguson had noticed the effect that missing out would have on Keane and Scholes, and indeed, on Henning Berg who was out injured. Ned Kelly was United's head of security, and Ferguson had instructed that he keep an eye on all three, Keane included. Such was the dedication in the Manchester United camp that even the security would make huge sacrifices, and Kelly ended up staying with the three players until the early hours of Wednesday morning. Everyone, regardless of whether they were playing or not, simply had to be looked after. All for one, and one for all!

A civic buffet was provided for all the players, staff, wives, and girlfriends, just like it had been after the FA Cup final. However, the difference was that on this occasion, the players could really let their hair down. It was mission accomplished. The night before the final had seen many of the players not get much sleep, but now many of them chose not to sleep at all as they partied into the small hours and beyond. Dwight Yorke had agreed to meet up with Jordi Cruyff, and off they went nightclubbing. Peter Schmeichel had ordered some of the finest Cuban cigars, and Yorkie had requested a Havana, to which his goalkeeper duly obliged, and he spent the night posing with it for several pictures. Posing was all that he would do, as he was not a smoker. It stayed with him all the way back to Manchester the next day, and it basically disintegrated on the team bus when once more, he tried to pose with it. Gary Neville found himself walking around the port of Barcelona the following morning with a bottle of Champagne in his hand. These are only a few stories—every player had a story to tell that night, and absolutely no one could blame them for not enjoying themselves.

They had rightfully earned it, and then some!

Perhaps the sweetest story of this entirely crazy night and following morning centred around David Beckham, and it occurred before the buffet. Becks was one of the last of the Manchester United contingent to leave the stadium, and after posing with the European Cup in the dressing room and going back on the pitch to reflect on what had just happened, he found himself as the unofficial custodian of the amazing trophy. As he left the stadium with the cup in tow to get on the coach, the first people that he bumped into were his parents, Sandra and Ted. It was a chance meeting as the plan was to meet back up at the hotel. If this was fate playing a major symphony, then it was opus rich. No words were spoken, as Becks placed the cup on the floor and just hugged his parents—a classic moment where no sound is made but there is shouting from the rooftops.

It wasn't just confined to those on the pitch where the stories and memories were made, everyone was in it together. Neil Custis was a sports journalist working for *The Sun*, covering the East Midlands. By his own admission, he was fortunate to get a ticket in the press box. A somewhat busman's holiday moment for the young reporter. Not expected to actually report on the game, Custis would gain valuable experience in how the press operate at such an exclusive game without him having to write down a single word. Custis explained exclusively for this book: "the sun was setting at a perfect time just before the match was to start. Montserrat Caballé was on the pitch performing the most apt of songs, and Freddie Mercury (who had passed away in November 1991) was on the big screens. I got goosebumps at the performance of Barcelona—a feeling shared with everyone in the stadium and all around the world. I'm really glad I wasn't working that evening as the game didn't really live up to expectation and I would have struggled to put down anything exciting to report on. There is an unwritten rule, especially in this country, that as a journalist, you cannot celebrate a goal. This is not the same on the continent, but when Sheringham scored the equaliser, I went into total rapture, punching the air. The more experienced hacks there would have disapproved of this. I really couldn't tell at the time, though, as I was so wrapped up in the moment. They didn't have time to haul me over the coals as Ole Gunnar Solskjaer put the ball into the Bayern net just moments later to give United the lead, and I was off again. I just couldn't help myself."

The next morning, Custis found himself at the airport and in the company of some of the finest sports reporters in the country. One of them was John Sadler, who was the chief football reporter at *The Sun*. The correspondent for the East

Midlands wanted more of this: "This is where I wanted to be from now on, and I was on a high. I called my girlfriend, Alicia, (who I soon married), and I was almost crying as I was regaling her with my experiences and recollections of a wonderful night in Barcelona. I was always an ambitious person, but this set me on course to where I really wanted to take my career. I wanted to cover the very best teams in the very best stadiums."

One of the journalists who may have raised his eyebrow at the Custis celebration was Peter Fitton, *The Sun* newspaper's Manchester United football correspondent. He would have been working on his match report as Neil Custis was taking in what he had witnessed on the pitch and in the Press Box. It would be one of Peter Fitton's last reports, as he was soon retiring. Custis would not have been aware of this as he boarded the plane back home, only that he now wanted bigger and better opportunities. That summer, Custis successfully applied for the role vacated by Fitton and he took a role as *The Sun's* Manchester United football correspondent at the start of the 1999–2000 season.

Neil Jones is a singer, writer, and musician. He is the frontman for an eight-piece blue-eyed soul band called *Stone Foundation*. The band have built a strong and solid fan base over the years and have recorded songs with some of the soul greats like Nolan Porter, William Bell, Bettye LaVette, and Melba Moore, as well as producing their own material. They have collaborated with former Dr Who, Peter Capaldi, and they also toured with *The Specials* and the Mod-Father himself, Paul Weller. The Mod-Father has also produced some of their albums as well. The band were formed in 1998, just as Manchester United were gearing up for the 1998–1999 season. Jones had a big love for music, which was matched only by his passion for his beloved United team, and he wanted the best of successes for his band and his team. He knew that he would have to work hard to become a full-time musician in 1999 and that he'd have to earn money elsewhere to fund his dream. And so, the young Jones took a job working for a German sunroof company whilst he maintained his dreams and aspirations. One day he was called into the office, and Jones takes up the story: "My mum's friend, Bruce, called me into his office to inform me that he'd acquired four tickets to the Champions League final via one of his German bosses and asked me if me and my dad would like to go! My feet couldn't carry me quick enough home to tell my dad we were going to Barcelona. We gathered around the family dining table and began to plan the trip of a lifetime. It was decided we'd have a week in Benidorm and then drive to Barcelona for the game, the perfect plan, the perfect holiday, and the perfect game."

"As we arrived at the airport on 22nd May, I knew I'd have to forfeit watching us go for the FA Cup. It was hard, but we were going to the Camp Nou, and by the time we'd landed in Spain, the flight attendant had informed us we'd won the game 2–0! What a start to our European adventure. Surely we were on the road to a ground-breaking treble?"

Jones continued, "As the days drew nearer to 26th May and the final my dad picked up the hire mini-bus and myself, my mum & dad, Bruce, his wife, and friend who was a Glasgow Rangers fan boarded the bus for the long drive to Barcelona. Driving in Spain is not for the faint-hearted! Especially when we reached the chaotic streets of Barcelona, so my dad used all of his driving experiences to navigate some near misses and deliver us safely to the hotel. Now it was time to head out onto Las Ramblas and it was a sea of red and white, it felt like we'd taken over the city, the atmosphere was joyous and carnival-like. Someone scaled one of the biggest statues on the street (even Fred Dibnah would have been proud of this feat) and placed an Eric Cantona mask on the statue's head. The songs continued all afternoon long and the beers and good-natured celebrations continued until it was time to head to the Camp Nou. We all squeezed onto the underground like sardines, and it was heart-in-mouth stuff as the underground train juddered and rocked under the strain of being overfilled. We finally piled out like sardines spilling into the street as we reached our destination. The scene of one of United's greatest ever nights. However, before that, we had to get into the ground, and it wasn't long after that we realised the tickets we have been given acquired by Bruce via his German sunroof company connections were in the Munich end!"

"A steward came to meet us and about 20 other United fans who had been held in a small area inside the stadium. He informed us that we couldn't sit in the German end wearing United shirts, so he would move us to the United end of the stadium. Those who went that day know that the Red Devils had over two thirds of the Camp Nou, the support was phenomenal.

The steward began to march us through the underground stadium bars through the German end of Camp Nou, our 20-strong party singing our hearts out as we went. The Germans tucked into their pre-match hot dogs and sauerkraut, watched open-mouthed as the steward led us straight through the middle of them. I don't think they could quite believe the cheek of it all as we sang our hearts out and headed towards our United brothers and sisters.

We finally emerged into the Spanish night air, level with the penalty area in the Manchester United end. We were told to sit in the row the steward signalled to, and he left us to get ready for the game. We started to watch the players warm up; my favourite part of this pre-match ritual with my dad was always to watch Peter Schmeichel warm up. When I was a kid, he'd always make sure we were in the Stretford End early to watch Kiddo (Brian Kidd) smack ball after ball towards the Great Dane as he swatted them back time after time to Brian's feet.

We were so wrapped up in the warm up we failed to see four United fans making their way down our row to their seats. The same seats the Spanish steward had placed us in! As we began to debate this conundrum, three or four Spanish police started wading into the rows in front of us with batons, shouting at any Manchester United supporter who was standing up and screaming 'sit down, sit down!' with each brutal swing of their hand-held clubs.

We'd seen their hit-first-and-ask-questions-later approach outside the ground earlier, and as they started swinging in our direction, we tried in vain to take our seats. Your main thought at an away game in Europe is always, 'if the baton doesn't get me, his gun definitely will!'

All I can say is as the game started, I was sat on the crack of two seats along with quite a few others on our row, waiting for the anger to subside, packed in but safe from the police batons. I've seen it at quite a few games abroad where peaceful English fans seem to be fair game for foreign police; maybe they see it as a badge of honour to attack English fans. I know we haven't helped ourselves over the years, but surely, they can see that a lot of us have changed from the boring old stereotype."

"The game started, the police faded away, and before you knew it, we're all standing again. What followed? Well, as United fans you all know the rest. Possibly the worst United performance I'd seen all year, missing Scholesy & Keano, we give Bayern chance after chance and head to the tunnel 1–0 down. The second half held even less optimism for us, and I remember turning to my dad saying: 'I can't believe we got all this way and didn't turn up!' and then suddenly all hell broke loose.

When the first went in from Teddy, we were jumping from row-to-row hugging strangers, shouting, 'it's extra-time, we've still got a chance.' Those words filled the air, and before we'd even taken another breath, Solskjaer had won it! Still to this day, it's the only time me and my dad have cried at a football match! The culmination of years and years of support, a father's love for his son, and the football club we both held so dear. Memories of the first time I came out of the tunnel on the Stretford End as a six-year-old holding my dad's hand; the sights the sounds of Sir Matt Busby Way; my first goal at Old Trafford, not feeling my feet touch the ground when we scored; my first away game at the Baseball Ground in Derby; European Cup nights; FA Cup victories; crushing defeats to old enemies; dreams of Robbo (Bryan Robson) lifting the title, and spending a season in the scoreboard paddock when King Eric (Cantona) came to rule the Premier League. All of those precious memories came out that night as me and my dad hugged and sobbed in the Spanish night air."

"We were European Champions, and forever United."

Mark Foster was a Manchester United fan working in the stadium that night. He was part of the club stewards and the security crowd, and he made sure an absolute club legend did not leave the ground at 1–0 down! Mark Foster explained, "We were instructed to leave with five minutes to go to get back to the coaches to escort the fans. If you look at the videos prior to Teddy's goal, you can see us all trailing out. I actually pushed George Best back through the gate as we rushed back to watch after my son called me, screaming down the phone that we had equalised. George thought it was all over and was off to the bar, but I dragged him back with us. We missed the second goal, and everyone jumped up in front of us as we came up stairs from the concourse. What an experience it was to be working and as a fan. I will never, ever forget it."

Another United fan, Ged Duffy, was working in sales and wanted to network more closely with his clients. Trouble was that he didn't play golf, and that's where the vast majority of his colleagues did their corporate entertaining. Ged's sales director had asked him what he would like to do as an alternative. Ged had stated that if he could get hold of a couple of tickets for the Champions League final, he would like to take a client and get the outlay back on corporate expenses. This was all agreed upon at 3 am at the company's annual conference in Southport on 4th January 1999—obviously, not knowing the line-up of the final, as Manchester United had not even played in the quarter-finals at this stage. Both Ged and his director had drank copious amounts of alcohol as they shook hands on this deal.

Ged had watched the semi-final second leg at home and was going crazy when the final whistle blew and United had made the final. Then reality set in for him as Ged explained, "How was I going to remind my boss what he had said in a drunken stupor some four months earlier? He won't remember, will he? At that moment the phone rang, and a familiar cockney voice asked me: 'Well, who are you taking then?' I was pleased that he had remembered."

The lucky client was Jimmy Ogden. Ged takes up the story once more, "I picked Jimmy up on the morning of the match near his house in Horwich, near Bolton, and we went to Manchester Airport. Once inside, we discovered that one of the three terminals had been allocated to Manchester United fans. On the departure screen, there was a plane leaving for Barcelona every 10 minutes, and there were dozens of Jumbo Jets parked on the tarmac, and as one plane departed, another one was towed into that bay."

"When we landed in Barcelona, the captain wouldn't let us off the plane until we all started singing 'Glory, Glory, Man United'. So, we duly obliged. When we got off the plane, we saw that he had a Manchester United flag flying out of his window and he was wearing a United bobble hat on his head. When we got outside the airport, there were free buses laid on to take us to the city centre.

On the bus, Jimmy told me that he would be paying for everything whilst in Barcelona. I told him that my sales director would want me to pay. He smiled and said: 'If you say no, Ged, I'll tell your boss that I had a rotten time here with you,' so I had to accept!

Once in the city centre, we decided to go on an open-top bus, which took us around half of the city and into the mountains to see the Olympic Stadium, which is home to Espanyol. On the way back, we passed a massive park and there was a game of football going on between United fans and Munich fans, it looked like it was 2,000 aside.

Along the route, we saw Manchester United fans everywhere, and when we got off the bus at Las Ramblas, it resembled Old Trafford on a match day. Every statue had a United hat, scarf, and banner hanging from it. The market stalls had Manchester United flags hanging from their roofs, and even the police motorbikes had United scarves tied to their aerials. It was a great party atmosphere, and despite all the warnings the bars were all open and doing great business.

We went to a restaurant and had a lovely meal. It was full of reds and Germans. It was a great atmosphere, no hint of trouble, with plenty of beer-driven songs being sung. I felt sorry for the Germans, as every one of them was wearing a Bayern scarf, woolly hat, and big coats, and the temperature was in the 30s (centigrade). After eating, we got on the Metro, and everywhere was full of reds—it looked like we had outnumbered them by at least three-to-one.

When we got to the famous Camp Nou, I was so disappointed as it resembled the outside of the Arndale Centre! The ground may have been a shithole outside, but as soon as I got inside, it took my breath away. You entered the stadium just below the top tier and then make your way down inside the lower tier, where we were sitting, as most of the stadium is actually below ground level.

When I got to ground level, I went to the pitch and just stood there looking around at this magnificent cathedral of football. I could see all four sides from this position, but when I got to Row 27 of Gol Nord 1 Graderia seat 20, I could only see the bottom bit of the opposite end and the bottom tier of the two sides. The view of the pitch was amazing."

"The seats were rigid, and the base did not fold up, but luckily there was enough room for two people between you and the seat in front, which came in very handy as there were two people for every seat in our section as so many had got into the stadium without tickets, so we stood for the whole game."

The match was nearing injury time as Ged continues his story: "Some German fans set off flares behind the other goal to celebrate; United had barely had a shot on target. The board went up, showing three minutes to go. Shit, just three minutes. Well, we've had a great day, and maybe it's not meant to be. Come on, boys. Please do something. Do anything. Hey, we've got a corner, and Schmeichel's coming up for it. Make it good Becks, please make it count."

Then Teddy Sheringham scores, and United have levelled the match.

"Utter pandemonium breaks out around three-quarters of the Camp Nou. I ended up about six or seven rows further down in the stand. I had to get back to my row. Great, made it. By the time I was back in my seat, we had another corner."

Ole Gunnar Solskjaer scores to give United the lead.

"Once again, I end up a few rows down as I see a guy fall from the tier above to luckily land on his back between two rows of seats. His fall was cushioned by a rucksack on his back. He got up and started screaming that all his beer in the rucksack has exploded and leaked. Two guys grabbed him and hoisted him on their shoulders. There was beer dripping everywhere, but he soon forgot his woes as he joined in the singing. I looked above me and the whole tier above was shaking, and I mean shaking. Outside the stadium, there were Germans lying on the ground everywhere crying their eyes out, while delirious United fans walk past them singing songs about Hitler and his one testicle and politely ask them where they were in 1945, totally politically incorrect nowadays, but not so in 1999."

"Back at the airport there were rows of Jumbo Jets lined up, 500 fans would be counted onto a plane, and it would leave. Then the next plane would pull in, and the next 500 would get on that plane. When I dropped Jimmy back at his house, he handed me all the receipts he had collected in Barcelona and told me to claim the money back from the company. I said no, but he demanded that I accept them. When I asked why he was doing this, he stated that he had never had a better football experience in his life, and he couldn't thank me enough."

Football 1 Golf 0!

Just like Ged Duffy, a number of fans had decided to travel to Barcelona on the day of the match. Andy Synnuck was one of them, and this time he didn't slap the thigh of the person who sat next to him, like he had done at Villa Park in the FA Cup semi-final. Andy takes up the story: "I had decided to drive up to stay in Manchester, the day before the final, and the flight was from Ringway Airport. Lots of beers were drunk, and it was a real fun night. My roommate who was older than me, retired at a sensible time knowing what we had in front of us. Let's just say exuberant youth was on my side, and there was no way I was giving in."

"Despite no sleep, I ran the whole day on adrenalin, basically. There was a great buzz at the airport as the charter flights departed. It was a sea of red, and I loved it. I was part of this dream, and I never wanted it to end."

"The craic on Las Ramblas, in the sun, with thousands of reds, was even better and we had some friendly with Bayern Munich fans. It was a carnival atmosphere and fair play to both sets of fans. We hit a few bars, as the beer flowed. My mate, Glenn, wisely said we line our stomachs as we would need to eat, otherwise, we'll never last the day. So, we found a nice tapas restaurant, but then that involved a few bottles of red wine. Outside the ground with friends, we bought some cans of beer from a street vendor. It was awful stuff and tasted like treacle, probably a barley wine of some sort, but strong, and did the job. We got into the ground, and the independent travel firm tickets were for the Bayern end. No drama, the fact that we HAD tickets was the main thing. We had a friendly word with security, as we were keen to have a peaceful safe final. They kindly escorted us to the Manchester United end, where I think they had provided an overflow capacity. We were so happy that we were in the United end. We had an aerial view, looking down the six-yard line across the box."

"True to United, things rarely go to plan, or ever straightforward, and Mario Basler put Bayern 1–0. Giggsy said afterwards they knew they didn't play well that night, understandably feeling leggy after a marathon season and also missing Keano and Scholesy. And so, the game drifted by, we became increasingly frustrated reds, and we were all asking how such a season could end as a damp squib, a bum note? I took my eyes off the game and looked skywards, reflecting on Sir Matt's birthday and my late father, saying a silent prayer to both. Please, send us some magic, we need it."

"When Teddy scored, pandemonium broke out. Grown men and women went completely nuts. I was lying on the concrete between the seats, at the bottom of a pile on. Screaming, shouting, yelling absolute nonsense. I hardly had chance to grasp my breath back, and from our vantage point, looking down that six-yard line, I saw Teddy's flick header and Ole instinctively sticking a boot out, but that doesn't do him justice. An intelligent goal scorer knew exactly what he was doing, and the ball flew off his boot like a bullet into the roof of the net. It was like a dagger to Bayern's heart. Again, there was chaos in our section, but I just sat there, partly in shock, partly soaking it all in. Glenn shook me roughly and screamed, 'f****** enjoy it!!'

'Oh, I am,' I calmly replied, welling up inside with emotion. One of those once-in-a-lifetime moments that not all football fans experience. We were the lucky ones."

"The final whistle blew. What the blazes have I just witnessed? Dreaming? Fantasizing? Did it really happen? I looked up to the sky, and I thanked Sir Matt and my dad. I do hope that they watched it together in Heaven! The squad paraded the trophy at the United end. Keano and Scholesy said they felt detached from that night—I guess a defence mechanism to curb their disappointment. The United fans were having none of it and made sure they lifted the trophy as part of the celebrations, and an acknowledgement to their contribution that season, not least of which was their performance in Turin a few weeks earlier."

"We went back to the airport knackered and emotional wrecks, but we didn't care. We had done it, and that's all that mattered to us. And that is all that mattered to everyone else as well."

CHAPTER EIGHTEEN
The 1998–1999 Season Overview

"Football. Bloody Hell!"
Alex Ferguson

***

1998

Game 1 v Arsenal (N) 9th August: Charity Shield—LOST 0–3

Game 2 v LKS Lodz (H) 12th August: UEFA Champions League Qualifier 1st Leg—WON 2–0
Giggs, Cole

Game 3 v Leicester City (H) 15th August: Premier League— DREW 2–2
Sheringham, Beckham

Game 4 v West Ham United (A) 22nd August: Premier League— DREW 0–0

Game 5 v LKS Lodz (A) 26th August: UEFA Champions League Qualifier 2nd Leg—DREW 0–0 (*United go through to the Champions League 2–0 on Aggregate*)

Game 6 v Charlton (H) 9th September: Premier League—WON 4–1
Solskjaer (2), Yorke (2)

Game 7 v Coventry (H) 12th September: Premier League—WON 2–0
Yorke, Johnsen

Game 8 v Barcelona (H) 16th September: UEFA Champions League Group D—DREW 3–3
Giggs, Scholes, Beckham

Game 9 v Arsenal (A) 20th September: Premier League—LOST 0–3

Game 10 v Liverpool (H) 24th September: Premier League—WON 2–0
Irwin (pen), Scholes

Game 11 v Bayern Munich (A) 30th September: UEFA Champions League Group D—DREW 2–2
Yorke, Scholes.

Game 12 v Southampton (A) 3rd October: Premier League—WON 3–0
Yorke, Cole, Cruyff.

Game 13 v Wimbledon (H) 17th October: Premier League—WON 5–1
Cole (2), Giggs, Beckham, Yorke.

Game 14: v Brondby (A) 21st October: UEFA Champions League Group D—WON 6–2
Giggs (2), Cole, Keane, Yorke, Solskjaer.

Game 15: v Derby County (A) 24th October: Premier League—DREW 1–1
Cruyff.

Game 16: v Bury (H) 28th October: League Cup Round 3—WON 2–0
Solskjaer, Nevland

Game 17: v Everton (A) 31st October: Premier League—WON 4–1
Yorke, Short (og), Cole, Blomqvist.

Game 18: v Brondby (H) 4th November: UEFA Champions League Group D—WON 5–0
Beckham, Cole, P Neville, Yorke, Scholes.

Game 19: v Newcastle United (H) 8th November: Premier League—DREW 0–0

Game 20: v Nottingham Forest (H) 11th November: League Cup Round 4—WON 2–1
Solskjaer (2).

Game 21: Blackburn Rovers (H) 14th November: Premier League—WON 3–2
Scholes (2), Yorke.

Game 22: v Sheffield Wednesday (A) 21st November: Premier League—LOST 1–3
Cole.

Game 23: v Barcelona (A) 25th November: UEFA Champions League Group D—DREW 3–3
Yorke (2), Cole.

Game 24: v Leeds United (H) 29th November: Premier League—WON 3–2
Solskjaer, Keane, Butt.

Game 25: v Tottenham Hotspur (A) 2nd December: League Cup Round 4—LOST 1–3
Sheringham.

Game 26: v Aston Villa (A) 5th December: Premier League—DREW 1–1
Scholes.

Game 27: v Bayern Munich (H) 9th December: UEFA Champions League Group D—DREW 1–1
Keane.

Game 28: v Tottenham Hotspur (A) 12th December: Premier League—DREW 2–2
Solskjaer (2).

Game 29: v Chelsea (H) 16th December: Premier League—DREW 1–1
Cole.

Game 30: v Middlesbrough (H) 19th December: Premier League—LOST 2–3
Butt, Scholes.

Game 31: v Nottingham Forest (H) 26th December: Premier League—WON 3–0
Johnsen (2), Giggs.

Game 32: v Chelsea (A) 29th December: Premier League—DREW 0–0

1999.

Game 33: v Middleborough (H) 3rd January: FA Cup Round 3—WON 3–1
Cole, Giggs, Irwin (pen).

Game 34: v West Ham United (H) 10th January: Premier League—WON 4–1
Yorke, Cole (2), Solskjaer.

Game 35: v Leicester City (A) 16th January: Premier League—WON 6–2
Yorke (3), Cole (2), Stam.

Game 36: v Liverpool (H) 24th January: FA Cup Round 4—WON 2–1
Yorke, Solskjaer.

Game 37: v Charlton Athletic (A) 31st January: Premier League—WON 1–0
Yorke.

Game 38: v Derby County (H) 3rd February: Premier League—WON 1–0
Yorke.

Game 39: v Nottingham Forest (A) 6th February: Premier League—WON 8–1
Yorke (2), Cole (2), Solskjaer (4).

Game 40: v Fulham (H) 14th February: FA Cup Round 5—WON 1–0
Cole.

Game 41: v Arsenal (H) 17th February: Premier League—DREW 1–1
Cole.

Game 42: v Coventry City (A) 20th February: Premier League—WON 1–0
Giggs.

Game 43: v Southampton (H) 27th February: Premier League—WON 2–1
Keane, Yorke.

Game 44: v Inter Milan (H) 3rd March: UEFA Champions League Quarter Final 1st Leg—WON 2–0
Yorke (2).

Game 45: v Chelsea (H) 7th March: FA Cup Quarter Final—DREW 0–0

Game 46: v Chelsea (A) 10th March: FA Cup Quarter Final Replay—WON 2–0
Yorke (2).

Game 47: v Newcastle United 13th March: Premier League—WON 2–1
Cole (2).

Game 48: v Inter Milan (A) 17th March: UEFA Champions League quarter-final 2nd Leg—DREW 1–1
Scholes. (United won 3–1 on aggregate)

Game 49: v Everton (H) 21st March: Premier League—WON 3–1
Solskjaer, Neville, Beckham.

Game 50: v Wimbledon (A) 3rd April: Premier League—DREW 1–1
Beckham.

Game 51: v Juventus (H) 7th April: UEFA Champions League semi-final 1st Leg—DREW 1–1
Giggs.

Game 52: v Arsenal (N) 11th April: FA Cup semi-final—DREW 0–0.

Game 53: v Arsenal (N) 14th April: FA Cup semi-final Replay—WON 2–1.
Beckham, Giggs.

Game 54: v Sheffield Wednesday (H) 17th April: Premier League—WON 3–0
Solskjaer, Sheringham, Scholes.

Game 55: v Juventus (A) 21st April: UEFA Champions League semi-final 2nd Leg—WON 3–2
Keane, Yorke, Cole (United won 4–3 on aggregate).

Game 56: v Leeds United (A) 27th April: Premier League—DREW 1–1
Cole.

Game 57: v Aston Villa (H) 1st May: Premier League—WON 2–1
Watson (og), Beckham.

Game 58: v Liverpool (A) 5th May: Premier League—DREW 2–2
Yorke, Irwin (pen).

Game 59: v Middlesbrough (A) 9th May: Premier League—WON 1–0
Yorke.

Game 60: v Blackburn Rovers (A) 12th May: Premier League—DREW 0–0

Game 61: v Tottenham Hotspur (H) 16th May: **Premier League Final**—WON 2–1
Beckham, Cole.

Game 62: v Newcastle United (N) 22nd May: **FA Cup Final**—WON 2–0
Sheringham, Scholes.

Game 63: v Bayern Munich (N) 26th May: **UEFA Champions League Final**—WON 2–1
Sheringham, Solskjaer.

Premier League—final table

Pos	Team	Pld	W	D	L	GF	GA	GD	Pts
1	Manchester United	38	22	13	3	80	37	43	79
2	Arsenal	38	22	12	4	59	17	42	78
3	Chelsea	38	20	15	3	57	30	27	75
4	Leeds United	38	18	13	7	62	34	28	67
5	West Ham United	38	16	9	13	46	53	-7	57
6	Aston Villa	38	15	10	13	51	46	5	55
7	Liverpool	38	15	9	14	68	49	19	54
8	Derby County	38	13	13	12	40	45	-5	52
9	Middlesbrough	38	12	15	11	48	54	-6	51
10	Leicester City	38	12	13	13	40	46	-6	49
11	Tottenham Hotspur	38	11	14	13	47	50	-3	47
12	Sheffield Wednesday	38	13	7	18	41	42	-1	46
13	Newcastle United	38	11	13	14	48	54	-6	46
14	Everton	38	11	10	17	42	47	-5	43
15	Coventry City	38	11	9	18	39	51	-12	42
16	Wimbledon	38	10	12	16	40	63	-23	42
17	Southampton	38	11	8	19	37	64	-27	41
18	Charlton Athletic	38	8	12	18	41	56	-15	36
19	Blackburn Rovers	38	7	14	17	38	52	-14	35
20	Nottingham Forest	38	7	9	22	35	69	-34	30

UEFA Champions League—
Group D final table

Pos	Team	Pld	W	D	L	GF	GA	GD	Pts
1	Bayern Munich	6	3	2	1	9	6	3	11
2	Manchester United	6	2	4	0	20	11	9	10
3	Barcelona	6	2	2	2	11	9	2	8
4	Brondby	6	1	0	5	4	18	-14	3

Appearances: 1998–1999 season

Player	League	W Cup	FA Cup	Europe	Total
Schmeichel	34	0	8	13	55
Neville G	34	0	7	12	53
Beckham	33 (1)	0 (1)	7	12	52 (2)
Keane	33 (2)	0	7	12	52 (2)
Stam	30	0	6 (1)	13	49 (1)
Yorke	32	0	5 (3)	11	48 (3)
Irwin	26 (3)	0	6	12	44 (3)
Cole	26 (6)	0	6 (1)	10	42 (7)
Scholes	24 (7)	0 (1)	3 (3)	10 (2)	37 (13)
Giggs	20 (4)	1	5 (1)	9	35 (5)
Butt	22 (9)	2	5	4 (4)	33 (13)
Neville (P)	19 (9)	2	4 (3)	4 (2)	29 (14)
Blomqvist	20 (5)	0 (1)	3 (2)	6 (1)	29 (9)
Johnsen	19 (3)	1	3 (2)	6 (2)	29 (7)
Berg	10 (6)	3	5	3 (1)	21 (7)
Solskjaer	9 (10)	3	4 (4)	1 (5)	17 (19)
Brown	11 (3)	0 (1)	2	3 (1)	16 (5)
Sheringham	7 (10)	1	1 (3)	2 (2)	11 (15)
May	4 (2)	2	1	0	7 (2)
van der Gouw	4 (1)	3	0	0	7 (1)
Curtis	1 (3)	3	0	0	4 (3)
Clegg	0	3	0	0	3
Cruyff	0 (5)	2	0	0 (3)	2 (8)
Wilson	0	2	0	0 (1)	2 (1)
Mulryne	0	2	0	0	2
Nevland	0	0 (1)	0	0	0 (1)
Notman	0	0 (1)	0	0	0 (1)
Wallwork	0	0 (1)	0	0	0 (1)

Goal Scorers: 1998–1999 season

Player	League	W Cup	FA Cup	Europe	Total
Yorke	18	0	3	8	29
Cole	17	0	2	5	24
Solskjaer	12	3	1	2	18
Scholes	6	0	1	4	11
Giggs	3	0	2	5	10
Beckham	6	0	1	2	9
Keane	2	0	0	3	5
Sheringham2	2	1	1	1	5
Irwin	2	0	1	0	3
Johnsen	3	0	0	0	3
Butt	2	0	0	0	2
Cruyff	2	0	0	0	2
Blomqvist	1	0	0	0	1
Neville G	1	0	0	0	1
Neville P	0	0	0	1	1
Nevland	0	1	0	0	1
Stam	1	0	0	0	1
Short (Everton)	1 (og)	0	0	0	1 (og)
Watson (Aston Villa)	1 (og)	0	0	0	1 (og)
Total	**80**	**5**	**12**	**31**	**128**

The curtain call at the end of the tour.

"The energy of live theatre is indescribable. You are just in the moment for an hour and a half."
Adrianne Palicki, American Actress.

***

David Beckham took the abuse and brunt of the nation's disappointment from France '98 and turned in some remarkable performances that highlighted his physical and mental strengths. There are not enough superlatives to describe his pinpoint-accurate crossing and the goals he scored. Think Tottenham in the last league game for the goal and the Champions League Final for his deliveries.

Henning Berg freed himself from previous injuries to form a formidable partnership with Jaap Stam, only to fall foul of injury towards the end of the campaign. This kept him out of the Champions League Final.

Jesper Blomqvist was waiting to reach his potential in his first year at the club but still provided some memorable moments on the left-hand side of United's attack when Ryan Giggs wasn't able to play there or, indeed, had taken on a more attacking role.

Wes Brown emerged as a very exciting player, full of ability, and one for the future.

Nicky Butt continued to show industry when he was called upon and never let the team down. His passing and movement off the ball developed, and he was a worthy replacement for Paul Scholes and Roy Keane.

Michael Clegg continued his progression and was used in League Cup games.

Andy Cole never gave up wanting to succeed in the United starting line-up, despite the fierce competition. He formed a great partnership with United's record signing, Dwight Yorke, both on and off the field. He scored the final goal of the league campaign to give United the title.

Jordi Cruyff proved himself to be a valuable member of the team when fit and contributed fine goals against Southampton and Derby. With competition so fierce in the attacking department, Cruyff accepted a loan spell with Celta Vigo later in the season.

Nick Culkin wasn't called upon for first team action, but was there ready and waiting.

John Curtis provided defensive strength when it was required despite having very limited team duties.

Ryan Giggs scored *the* goal of the season in that FA Cup semi-final at Villa Park against United's closest rivals, Arsenal. His performances at times reached brilliant heights, and he could adapt to life on the left wing and upfront with ease.

Raimond van der Gouw spent the vast majority of the season as understudy to Peter Schmeichel but performed admirably when called upon on the pitch and as a goalkeeping coach.

Jonathan Greening was part of the squad in Barcelona and was one for the future with his pace and skill.

Danny Higginbotham played all his senior football for Royal Antwerp in Belgium as he knew his chances of getting into the first team were slim.

Dennis Irwin turned 33 during the campaign yet showed absolutely no sign of any decline in his play and commitment to overlapping and defending. He kept the young guns at bay.

Ronny Johnsen continued to show why he was such an important member of the squad in his versatility to produce the results in defence and midfield when called upon.

Roy Keane was simply 'Captain Fantastic' all season and produced some inspiring football. None more so than in the Champions League semi-final in Turin. An early booking made him and everyone else aware that he would be missing the final. He put this behind him to lead the team to glory. Awe-inspiring.

David May found his opportunities limited due to his colleagues' shining in defence as well as injuries. He performed admirably when called upon.

Gary Neville cemented his place at right-back and also in central defence when required. Like Dennis Irwin, he was superb at the overlap and linked up brilliantly with his mate, David Beckham.

Phil Neville did not get the game time like his brother, Gary, but reminded Dennis Irwin to keep on his toes at left-back. He also played in midfield when called upon.

Erik Nevland would also play his part when called upon, but like Jordi Cruyff, he found himself falling down the pecking order, and he too went out on loan with Swedish Club, IFK Gothenburg.

Alex Notman would only feature in one game in the league cup defeat at Tottenham Hotspur before going out on loan to Aberdeen in Scotland.

Peter Schmeichel didn't start the season too well and decided to leave Old Trafford at the end of the year. This weighed heavily on his mind until it was finally announced, and then he ended up being the hero of *the* defining match of the season at Villa Park in the FA Cup semi-final and captained the team to European glory in his final match for United.

Paul Scholes continued his journey in proving that he was one of the most elite and complete central midfielders in the country. He played with heart, intelligence, and contributed to the cause with some very important goals. Like Roy Keane, he too missed the Champions League final due to suspension. His place as one of the most important players in the team was already well assured.

Teddy Sheringham found himself at the wrong end of ridicule from the South as he did not win any trophies with United in his first season. He also found himself on the bench more times than he would have liked at the age of 31. However, his contributions when called upon were exemplary, none more so in the FA Cup and Champions League finals.

Ole Gunnar Solskjaer, like Sheringham, found himself regularly sitting on the bench. The difference was that he was younger and learning his trade. His contributions from the bench increased as the season wore on, especially against Nottingham Forest away in the league when he came on and scored four goals in an 8–1 victory. He scored a last-minute goal in the fourth round of the FA Cup at home to Liverpool to give United the win after they had been a goal down for much of the game. He also did the same in the Champions League final as well!

Jaap Stam started his United career with a few below-par games but soon became the kingpin in the heart of the United defence, forming great partnerships with Johnsen and Berg.

Michael Twiss continued his education by going out on loan at Sheffield United, where he played under United legend Steve Bruce.

Ronnie Wallwork found himself down the pecking order and, like a few of the players in his position, decided that a loan move would aid his game, and he joined Danny Higginbotham at Royal Antwerp.

Mark Wilson was coming through the ranks, and he made one substitute appearance, coming on against Brondby in the Champions League Group game in Denmark.

Dwight Yorke proved all his doubters wrong. His smile lit up Old Trafford as he became the leading goal scorer for United in all competitions and formed great relationships with whomever he partnered in attack, especially with Andy Cole alongside him.

A formidable ensemble of the finest performers, with a brilliant supporting cast who could step up onto the stage and deliver their lines just as well when they were required to. Always to standing ovations and wonderful reviews, with mostly five stars given:

Matinée or Evenings.
A show of epic proportions immaculately
directed by Alex Ferguson
and produced effortlessly by
Brian Kidd (and later, Steve McLaren).
The hottest ticket in town!

CHAPTER NINETEEN
The Following Season: 1999–2000

The morning after (the night before)
An English Idiom.

***

JUST EXACTLY HOW do you follow up the greatest season in Manchester United's history? A season so unique in its execution. United had won a historic treble of the Premier League, FA Cup, and Champions League. No club in England had done this previously. Andy Cole has since been asked this question in interviews. To this day, he concedes that the plan was always to make sure they did it again. He jokes that his strike partner, Dwight Yorke, asked for a year off! 'That's Yorkie, that's Peter Pan for you.'

Manchester United were unique and always have been. It had even made HM The Queen sit up and take notice, and it was no surprise when Alex Ferguson was knighted for his services. The Prime Minister, Tony Blair, had been calling for it, as had many others in the footballing world. The Queen announced Ferguson's knighthood in her Birthday Honours list in June 1999. "I am delighted and honoured," said the United manager after finding out. "I see this as an honour, and not just for me but for the people who have supported me all my life and made me what I am. Manchester United's success is not just down to me but to the players who have to deliver on the pitch and to the people of Old Trafford, past and present, who have made it the greatest football club in the world. I want to thank my brother Martin and my three sons for their constant love and support. Above all, I want to thank my wife, Cathy. She knows better than anyone the pressures of the job and the demands they place on me. She is the rock of stability in my life, and I share this honour with her."

Peter Kenyon, deputy chief executive, also offered praise on behalf of the club, saying, "Everyone at Manchester United is delighted by the news. It is a fantastic accolade and honour for a man who has put in so much hard work and determination, not only at Manchester United but also for British football. I couldn't think of a more befitting way to end what has been an unbelievable season."

On 22nd July 1999, Ferguson was awarded his knighthood by The Queen. It would sit beside his OBE. He would also be following in the footsteps of Sir Matt Busby, who had been knighted by The Queen in 1968.

Arise, Sir Alex Ferguson!

For the second successive season, United would become embroiled in matters that concerned the FA and the Government. There would be new competitions for United to compete in on the world stages, but perhaps the biggest story of the 1999–2000 season was the competition that they would not enter.

On the transfer front, Erik Nevland returned to his native Norway with Viking Stavanger. The other departures included Richard Wellens to Blackpool, Michael Twiss to Port Vale, and John Curtis to Blackburn for a fee of £1.5 million.

The biggest-named departure was Peter Schmeichel, who joined the Portuguese club Sporting, and Mark Bosnich was brought in to replace him. Bosnich was no stranger to Manchester United. In his youth, the Australian shot-stopper was at United from 1989 to 1991. During that time, he played for the senior team three times. After a stint in his home country playing for Sydney United during the 1991–1992 season, Bosnich found himself back in the Northern Hemisphere. This time, it would be with Aston Villa, where he made his way into the number one spot and kept it. He was with Villa from 1992 to 1999, when Bosnich saw his contract out, and therefore the move to United was a free transfer.

The return to United had not been the successful one that he and the club had hoped for, though. A loss of form and injuries meant that Bosnich would play just 23 league games; Raimond van der Gouw, 11, and Massimo Taibi, who joined from Venezia for £4.5 million, started just four. With Schmeichel in goal, United had possessed a recognised and strong number one. The 1999–2000 season would be one of transition for United in this department, with headlines centred around some high-profile gaffes on the back pages. One such headline was "Blind Venetian" after Taibi allowed a very weak shot by Matt Le Tissier to slip through his legs in a game against Southampton in September 1999.

Outside of the goalkeeping berth, United also acquired South African midfielder Quinton Fortune from Atletico Madrid for a fee of £1.5 million. And the defence was bolstered by the signing of Mikael Silvestre. The Frenchman had spent the previous year at Inter Milan, and that was enough to convince Sir Alex to spend £4 million to acquire his services. Liverpool had also made an approach for the French international, but to no avail.

After all the pre-season matches had been completed, United again faced Arsenal in the Charity Shield at Wembley, and the Gunners once again claimed victory. This time the score was 2–1. Dwight Yorke had given United a half-time lead, but a Kanu penalty in the 67th and a goal from Ray Parlour in the 78th minute sealed the win for the Gunners.

On 27th August 1999, United played Lazio in the UEFA Super Cup. United were European champions; the Italians had won the European Cup Winners' Cup. The game was played at the Stade Louis II in Monaco, with Lazio winning the game by 1–0 courtesy of a goal from their Chilean striker, Marcelo Salas. It was the last time that the winners of the European Cup Winners' Cup would play in the Super Cup. From 2000, the winners of the UEFA Cup took on the European Cup holders for the Super Cup title.

There was also to be no joy in the League Cup again, with United going out in the third round with a 3–0 away to Aston Villa.

Manchester United added their first trophy of the season on 30th November 1999, claiming the Intercontinental Cup when they played the Brazilian club, Palmeiras. The game took place at the National Stadium in Tokyo in front of 53,372 people. United were playing as European champions, and Palmeiras had the honour of being the winners of the 1999 Copa Libertadores, South America's premier club championship. Roy Keane scored the only goal in the 35th minute.

Changes were made to the UEFA Champions League for the 1999–2000 season as an additional group round was added. The first round would consist of 32 teams with eight groups of four, and then the additional round would consist of 16 teams with four groups of four. This meant that the top two clubs in the second qualifying round would participate in the quarter-final and the competition would revert back to its knockout format.

The first group stage once more saw United placed in Group D; the only difference from the year before was that it wasn't quite the Group of Death. Instead of facing Barcelona, Bayern Munich, and Brondby, the holders were drawn against Marseille from France, Sturm Graz from Austria, and the Croatian team, Croatia Zagreb. As expected, United topped the group, winning four and drawing one before losing 1–0 to second-placed Marseille.

The second group stage draw saw Manchester United in Group B, along with Valencia, Fiorentina, and Bordeaux. Again, United topped the group with four wins, one draw, and a defeat in the opening group game, 2–0 away to Fiorentina.

So far, so good for the defending champions—two group rounds successfully executed and in pole position as well. Now it was back to the knockout stages.

The seven other teams that joined United were Real Madrid, Porto, Bayern Munich, Valencia, Lazio, Chelsea, and Barcelona. United were paired with Real Madrid, who would provide the holders with a very stern test. The Real Madrid squad was a who's who of the finest stars in world football at the time. The Galácticos included the likes of Iker Casillas, Roberto Carlos, Ivan Campo, Christian Karembeu, Clarence Seedorf, and Raúl, to name a few. Steve McManaman, formerly of Liverpool, was also playing on the right side of Real Madrid's midfield to add even more spice into the mix.

Manchester United had home advantage in the second leg as a reward for topping their second group stage. Real Madrid were runners-up in theirs to Bayern Munich in Group C. The first leg was held at the Santiago Bernabéu in Madrid on 4th April 2000. The match ended goalless. Whilst an away goal would have been useful, United could feel that they had put a shift in taming the home team. The second leg would be an entirely different game!

Two weeks later, 60,000 fans packed into Old Trafford for the return leg. The pace of the game was immense, with the Spanish giants taking the game to United even though Ryan Giggs fired wide in the early seconds of the match. Raúl and Roberto Carlos on the right-hand side were causing problems for the home team, and Madrid came close to taking the lead in the 13th minute of the match. Hesitancy from Fernanda Morientes when he was free charging down in the box allowed Raimond van der Gouw to get down and prevent Madrid from taking the lead. The Old Trafford faithful breathed a huge collective sigh of relief. It didn't last long, though, as in the 20th minute, disaster struck for United. Morientes was causing the home team problems, and he hit a fine ball to Iván Helguera. Roy Keane was backtracking and put the ball into his own net. First blood to Real Madrid.

This brought Manchester United to life, with both Dwight Yorke and Ryan Giggs coming close. If United had gone in at the break still very much in the game, then they were well and truly out of it at the early stages of the second half. Two goals, both scored by Raul, in the 50th and 52nd minutes put paid to any hopes of United retaining their status as European champions. A valiant attempt was made when Manchester United scored in the 64th minute, a brilliant individual goal from David Beckham, and then a penalty in the 88th minute converted by Paul Scholes made the score respectable. The damage had been done, though, and Real Madrid went through 3–2 on aggregate. It was Spain 2, England 0, as Barcelona put Chelsea out at the same stage. Real Madrid went on to win the final 3–0 against Valencia. An all-Spanish final, with English man Steve McManaman scoring a spectacular goal.

United drew the first game of their Premier League season on 8th August 1999, as they had done the previous season, only this time it was away to Everton. Dwight Yorke had given the champions the perfect start when he scored his first goal of the season in only the seventh minute. It looked like it would be enough for all three points until Jaap Stam put the ball into his own net with just four minutes remaining to salvage a point for Everton.

Three days later, and the first home game of the season, against Sheffield Wednesday, saw United run rampant in front of a crowd just shy of 55,000. Paul Scholes and Dwight Yorke put United in control in the first half before Andy Cole and Solskjaer opened up their accounts for the season. A comprehensive 4–0 victory ensured that United moved up into third place in the league. They hit the top spot just a few days later when they entertained Leeds United at Old Trafford. A brace from Dwight Yorke in the 77th and 80th minute, with no reply from their Yorkshire rivals. It was Yorke's fourth goal in the three games, proving that he was no one-season wonder.

Manchester United went on to win their next four games in the league, maintaining their position at the summit. Crucially, during this period, there were wins against Arsenal and Liverpool. The 2–1 win against the Gunners was even more special as United had not beaten Arsenal in the league for the past two seasons. Coventry City and Newcastle United were despatched before United won away at Liverpool by 3–2. The next two games were at Old Trafford, and on paper, it looked like United would continue their winning streak. However, they would take a point apiece, first with a 1–1 draw with Wimbledon and then sharing six goals against Southampton. It was four points dropped, but United still held the top spot.

They would drop down to second place in the next game, when they were comprehensively beaten at Stamford Bridge by a rampant Chelsea side who stuck the ball in the United goal five times without reply. This had been their first defeat in the league since a 3–2 home defeat against Middlesbrough back in December 1998. The next away game also bought Manchester United defeat, and once more this would be in London when they lost 3–1 at White Hart Lane to a very good Tottenham Hotspur team. United dropped to third in the league. This was the lowest they would go, and they returned back to the top of the table on 6th November 1999, when they beat Leicester City at the 'Theatre of Dreams', 2–0, with Andy Cole scoring a brace.

The Red Devils only lost the top spot on one more occasion

as they romped to their second successive league title, winning their last 11 games in the process. In claiming the title, United had amassed a record Premier League goals tally of 97 and had finished the season an incredible 18 points ahead of their nearest rivals, Arsenal. There would be no last-day nerves this time around. This feat was even more impressive as Manchester United's rivals had all spent big in order to at least match them. There were still two more trophies for United to challenge for in the 1999–2000 season—or so we thought!

The 2000 FIFA Club World Championship was the inaugural FIFA Club World Cup and was played from 5th January to 14th January 2000 in two stadiums in Brazil. These were either Rio de Janeiro's, Estadio do Maracanã, or São Paulo's, Estadio do Morumbi. Apparently, Brazil had been selected to host the tournament as far back as September 1997. In total, eight teams would be competing for the trophy. The competition was made up of two teams from South America, two from Europe, and one each from North America, Africa, Asia, and Oceania. The teams were:

Corinthians who qualified as the 1998 Campeonato Brasileiro.
Al-Nassr as winners of the 1998 Asian Super Cup.
Manchester United for winning the 1998–1999 UEFA Champions League.
Club Necaxa as winners of the 1999 CONCACAF Champions Cup.
Raja Casablanca as winners of the 1999 CAF Champions League.
Real Madrid as winners of the 1998 Intercontinental Cup.
South Melbourne as winners of the 1999 Oceania Club Championship
Vasco da Gama as winners of the 1998 Copa Libertadores

The format consisted of two groups of four playing three games each, with the top two competing in the final. The runners-up would contest the third-place play-off.

United finished third in Group B and didn't qualify for either. They drew their first game 1–1 against Club Necaxa before losing 3–1 to Vasco da Gama. They salvaged some pride with a

2–0 win against Australian side, South Melbourne. The eventual winners were Corinthians, who beat Vasco da Gama on penalties in an all-Brazilian final. The Mexican team, Club Necaxa, took third place when they beat Real Madrid in a penalty shootout.

If the actual tournament itself didn't fill many column inches, then the build-up to it most certainly did! In fact, it is subject to an often-used pub quiz question:

Who knocked Manchester United out of the FA Cup in the 1999–2000 season?

Of course, the answer is no one. Manchester United didn't compete in the FA Cup that year!

At the time, the FA and the Government were preparing to bid for the 2006 World Cup, and a whole host of football dignitaries were involved. As the author of this book, I got to witness one of these events first-hand. In February 2000, I happened to be on the same flight to São Paulo as Sir Bobby Charlton and the Sports Minister at the time, Tony Banks. After shaking hands with Sir Bobby, he then went on to tell me about the presentations and proposals that he was involved in. The details were sparing and most definitely on a 'need to know' basis, but it was enough for me just to shake his hand and be in his presence.

The Government and the FA were adamant that it would be "in the nation's interest" for Manchester United to participate in the FIFA Club World Cup. It was thought to be an asset in winning the bid to host the 2006 World Cup, but something would have to give, and that something was going to be the FA Cup. The very same FA Cup that United had won the previous season. It was concluded that there was no way that United could participate in both competitions.

Therefore, the pressure grew on Manchester United, and in many pubs and clubs across the country, the terrace talk turned to "will they, or won't they?" In one corner it was the 2006 World Cup bid group, and in the other were the football purists and traditionalists. Could the third round of the FA Cup, which has always been played in the first week of January, be played later that month? Could United just field the reserves? The oldest cup competition was in serious danger of becoming devalued, whichever way one looked at it.

The question was soon answered, and this is how *The*

Guardian reported the announcement. "Manchester United announced this afternoon that they are withdrawing from next season's FA Cup. The decision is subject to contractual issues, which still have to be resolved. In a statement, the club said: 'We realise that many of our supporters will be as disappointed as we are with our decision not to compete in the FA Cup. Manchester United see this as an opportunity to compete for the ultimate honour of being the very first World Club Champions.' The Football Association offered to exempt the FA Cup holders from the competition in a bid to persuade them to play in the FIFA World Team Championship in Brazil in January and so help England's 2006 World Cup bid. That left United in a no-win situation, knowing that they would disappoint their fans if they agreed to pull out of the FA Cup and disappoint the FA and the Government if they refused to play in Brazil. United agonised over their decision for two days before announcing at an Old Trafford press conference that they had reluctantly agreed to accept the FA's offer."

Manchester United had defied opposition from supporters of not only their own club but of other clubs as well by agreeing to participate in the FIFA Club World Cup at the expense of the FA Cup. The decision sent shock waves across the football community, causing consternation and anger in very equal measures.

The BBC also reported that United chairman, Martin Edwards, said the club had "no alternative" but to accept the offer for one year only. "We can't go for them all," he said. "We can't play in the FA Cup and in Brazil. That would be impossible. We're in a no-win situation here. The criticism we would have received if we hadn't gone [to Brazil] would have been unthinkable—and that's a Scotsman speaking."

It may have been announced at the end of June 1999, but the conversations continued right up to the draw for the third round, and there was a glimmer of hope that something could be done. When the newly appointed Sports Minister, Kate Hoey, criticised the club for the way it was treating its fans, it compelled Sir Alex Ferguson to set the record straight. Sir Alex had never wanted United to opt-out of the FA Cup, and he wanted his players to defend it. *The Guardian* reported on Thursday 28th

October 1999, that "Ferguson picked up his mobile phone, punched in a number, and was straight through to Tony Blair, who was at a conference on the bombing of Kosovo. 'Blair was not too pleased, but neither was Ferguson,' said a source. The fact that Ferguson was able to call the Prime Minister on his mobile phone shows the importance attached to United's participation in the FA Cup and the implications of the decision to withdraw. Over the past few weeks, attempts to negotiate an agreement that would allow the club to take part in the FA Cup and in next year's inaugural World Club Championship have involved Mr. Blair, Ms. Hoey, the Culture and Sports Secretary, Chris Smith, and representatives of players and football organisations. *The Guardian* has learned that the Premier League offered to extend the football season by up to 10 days to allow United to participate in the cup, but this was rejected by the Football Association and the club's directors. A source said the FA 'didn't want an extension because of the European Championships next summer and because they felt that it would be unfair to other clubs.'"

The Guardian article went on, "'A follow-up offer to extend the season for all English clubs in European competitions was similarly rejected. It was a genuine offer and a genuine way of getting around the problem,' said the source. It was controversial in its implications for other clubs, and both the FA and United moved pretty quickly to reject it. Whilst the manager and the players were looking at it from a football viewpoint, there were others looking at it from a fiscal one. Leading players such as captain Roy Keane have expressed their opposition to the withdrawal to the Professional Footballers Association, which has intervened on their behalf. However, while Manchester United FC want to defend the world's most prestigious cup, Manchester United PLC are trying to cash in on the opportunity to play in a global tournament in Brazil. Football finance analyst, Simon Banks, said, 'United stand to make millions of pounds through the global exposure they will receive by participating in Brazil, much more than can be made in the FA Cup. It's a great opportunity for the club to spread the brand name. United are opening club shops around the world. So, whilst Manchester United basked in

May 1999 glory (and rightly so), it would bring its problems towards the end of the year.'"

In the end, Manchester United did not participate in the FA Cup. They did not win the FIFA Club World Cup either, and England were not awarded the World Cup in 2006, so what was the whole point of the exercise? Germany were chosen to host the 2006 World Cup.

The only real winner was Darlington. They had been beaten by Gillingham in the second round of the FA Cup but became the lucky losers who would take Manchester United's place in the third round and were rewarded with a money-spinning trip to Aston Villa, where they were narrowly beaten 2–1.

So that was the 1999–2000 season for Manchester United. It was an almost impossible task to replicate what had taken place the season before. United were majestic in the league but were used as pawns in a political gamble that did not pay off, entering new competitions that were truly worldwide, and not entering old competitions in their own backyard!

Manchester United were involved in a number of different competitions during that season, and here is how they finished in them.

FA Premier League

Pos	Team	Pld	W	D	L	GF	GA	GD	Pts
1	Manchester United	38	28	7	3	97	45	52	91
2	Arsenal	38	22	7	9	73	43	30	73
3	Leeds United	38	21	6	11	58	43	15	69
4	Liverpool	38	19	10	9	51	30	21	67
5	Chelsea	38	18	11	9	53	34	19	65
6	Aston Villa	38	15	13	10	46	35	11	58
7	Sunderland	38	16	10	12	57	45	1	58
8	Leicester City	38	16	7	15	55	55	0	55
9	West Ham United	38	15	10	13	52	53	-1	55
10	Tottenham Hotspur	38	15	8	15	57	49	8	53
11	Newcastle United	38	14	10	14	63	54	9	52
12	Middlesbrough	38	14	10	14	46	52	-6	52
13	Everton	38	12	14	12	59	49	10	50
14	Coventry City	38	12	8	18	47	54	-7	44
15	Southampton	38	12	8	18	45	62	-17	44
16	Derby County	38	9	11	18	44	47	-13	38
17	Bradford City	38	9	9	20	38	68	-30	36
18	Wimbledon	38	7	12	19	46	74	-28	33
19	Sheffield Wednesday	38	8	7	23	38	70	-32	31
20	Watford	38	6	6	26	35	77	-42	24

FIFA Club World Cup

Pos	Team	Pld	W	D	L	GF	GA	GD	Pts
1	Vasco da Gama	3	3	0	0	7	2	5	9
2	Necaxa	3	1	1	1	5	4	1	4
3	Manchester United	3	1	1	1	4	4	0	4
4	South Melbourne	3	0	0	3	1	7	-6	0

UEFA Champions League—First Stage: Group D

Pos	Team	Pld	W	D	L	GF	GA	GD	Pts
1	Manchester United	6	4	1	1	9	4	5	13
2	Marseille	6	3	1	2	10	8	2	10
3	Sturm Graz	6	2	0	4	5	12	-7	6
4	Croatia Zagreb	6	1	2	3	7	7	0	5

UEFA Champions League—Second Stage: Group B

Pos	Team	Pld	W	D	L	GF	GA	GD	Pts
1	Manchester United	6	4	1	1	10	4	6	13
2	Valencia	6	3	1	2	9	5	4	10
3	Fiorentina	6	2	2	2	7	8	-1	8
4	Bordeaux	6	0	2	4	5	14	-9	2

Player Appearances

Player	League	W Cup	Europe	World Championship	Other	Total
Bosnich	23	1	7	2	2	35
Neville G	22	0	9	2	2	35
Irwin	25	0	13	2	2	42
May	0 (1)	0	1	0	0 (1)	1 (2)
Johnsen	2 (1)	0	0	0	0	2 (1)
Stam	33	0	13	2	3	51
Beckham	30(1)	0	12	1 (1)	3	46 (2)
Butt	21 (11)	0	4 (2)	2	2	29 (13)
Cole	23 (5)	0	13	2	2	40 (5)
Sheringham	15 (12)	0	6 (3)	0 (2)	1 (2)	19 (22)
Giggs	30	0	11	2	1	44
Neville P	25 (4)	0	6 (3)	2(1)	2	35 (8)
Curtis	0 (1)	1	0	0	0 (1)	1 (2)
Cruyff	1 (7)	1	1 (3)	1 (1)	1 (1)	5 (12)
Keane	28 (1)	0	12	2	2	44 (1)
van der Gouw	11 (3)	0	7	1	1	20 (3)
Scholes	27 (4)	0	11	0	3	41 (4)
Yorke	29 (3)	0	9 (2)	2	1 (1)	41 (6)
Solskjaer	15 (13)	1	4 (7)	2 (1)	2 (1)	24 (22)
Berg	16 (6)	0	11 (1)	1	2	30 (7)
Clegg	0 (2)	1	1 (1)	0	0	2 (3)
Fortune	4 (2)	0	1 (3)	1 (1)	0	6 (6)
Taibi	4	0	0	0	0	4
Silvestre	30 (1)	0	2 (2)	2	1	35 (3)
Higginbotham	2 (1)	1	0 (1)	1	0	4 (2)
Wallwork	0 (5)	1	0	1	0	2 (5)
Culkin	0 (1)	0	0	0	0	0 (1)
Wilson	1 (2)	0	2 (1)	1	0	4 (3)
Greening	1 (3)	1	1 (1)	1	0 (1)	4 (5)
O'Shea	0	1	0	0	0	1
Healy	0	0 (1)	0	0	0	0 (1)
Chadwick	0	1	0	0	0	1
Wellens	0	0 (1)	0	0	0	0 (1)
Twiss	0	1	0	0	0	1
Rachubka	0	0	0	0 (1)	0	0 (1)

Goalscorers

Player	League	W Cup	Europe	World Championship	Other	Total
Irwin	3	0	0	0	0	3
Beckham	6	0	2	0	0	8
Butt	3	0	0	1	0	4
Cole	19	0	3	0	0	22
Sheringham	5	0	1	0	0	6
Giggs	6	0	1	0	0	7
Cruyff	3	0	0	0	0	3
Keane	5	0	6	0	1	12
Scholes	9	0	3	0	0	12
Yorke	20	0	2	1	1	24
Solskjaer	12	0	3	0	0	15
Fortune	2	0	0	2	0	4

CHAPTER TWENTY
Manchester United into the Millennium: 2001–2008

'Stars Directing Fate'
Robbie Williams, Guy Chambers, Leslie Bricusse, John Barry

***

AT THE DAWN of the 1990s, Liverpool had dominated the previous decade and were the team to beat and emulate from any competition. However, by the start of the 21st Century, it was Manchester United's turn to lead, whilst everyone else seemingly followed.

In the early to mid-part of the 1990s, it was Aston Villa, Blackburn Rovers, and Newcastle United that provided the sternest of challenges to the United throne. Blackburn did in fact breach the Red Wall in 1995 when they became Champions of England, while Villa and Newcastle (twice) tried in vain but came off second best. If Manchester United had not been thwarted in 1995, it would have meant that they would finish at the top of the summit for five consecutive seasons. Even Liverpool hadn't done that with the dominance afforded to them in the 1970s and 1980s.

The latter part of the 1990s saw Arsenal emerge as the dominant force who could stop United and knock them off their perch. Arsenal had been crowned Champions in 1998, and as the early years of the 2000s commenced, there would be a time when the reds from Manchester and the reds from North London would swap positions. In 2001, United were crowned Champions for the third season in a row, but the title swung back in favour of Arsenal in the following year, and then back to United the season after. In the 2003–2004 season, Arsenal took the crown back in a remarkable year which saw the Gunners go through the entire season in the league without a single defeat and were named the 'Invincibles'.

Watching events closely, just a few miles from North London, were Chelsea. The club was purchased in 2003 by Roman Abramovich. Upon receipt of buying the West London club, it became very apparent just how seriously rich the Russian Oligarch was, and very soon they would find themselves dining on the top table of not only English football but also European football greatness themselves.

The deal to buy Chelsea was announced at the start of July 2003. This is how the BBC reported it on 2nd July in their business section. "Chelsea Football Club is to be bought by Russian billionaire Roman Abramovich in a deal worth £140 million. The surprise takeover—the biggest in British football history—was finalised late on Tuesday after talks with long-time chairman Ken Bates. He bought the club in 1982 for just £1, while taking on debts of £1.5 million. Although the club has prospered, debts have grown, and it is estimated the new owner will stump up £80 million to cover them. On top of that, Mr Abramovich is buying just over half the shares of Chelsea Village, which owns the football club, for 35p each—putting the total value of the club's shares at £59.3 million. The Russian businessman pledged to plough even more resources into the club while Mr Bates said the deal would move Chelsea onto the 'next level.'

Meanwhile, Mr Abramovich told the BBC, 'We are delighted to agree this deal to acquire what is already one of the top clubs in Europe. We have the resources and ambition to achieve even more given the huge potential of this great club.'"

The BBC then went on to discuss the new owner's business attributes outside of football, "Mr Abramovich is one of the major shareholders in Sibneft (now Gazprom), one of Russia's largest oil companies, and 'a keen follower of sport and international football', a statement said. Mr Abramovich also has significant interests in Russia's aluminium industry, and until recently, owned a sizeable stake in Russian airline Aeroflot—the sale of which may have funded the Chelsea buyout."

And just like in September 1998 with the proposed takeover of United by Rupert Murdoch, it may have made the shareholders happy, but not on the terraces or in Parliament. One Chelsea fan told the BBC he was shocked by the news: "I think it's disgraceful because I always thought that Ken Bates was Mr. Chelsea." Meanwhile, former Sports Minister, Tony Banks, said he wanted more information on Mr. Abramovich's business background, "I want to know whether this individual is a fit and proper person to be taking over a club like Chelsea. Until that question is answered, then I'm afraid the jury is out," he told the BBC. Mr. Banks added, "A sale has been arranged to an individual we know nothing about." He also said that he would be raising the issue with the Sports Minister, Richard Caborn. However, Ken Bates, who was expected to remain as chairman, told the BBC the deal would help the club. "This is a great deal for Chelsea Village, the club, and its fans," he said in a statement. "In today's highly competitive football market, the club will benefit from a new owner with deeper pockets to move Chelsea to the next level. I look forward to working with Roman Abramovich to achieve even greater things." The BBC closed the article with a statement that would have made investors happy, "Chelsea Village shares were up 12p to 40p in early trading on Wednesday."

This deal to buy Chelsea heralded the start of major investment from overseas and changed football in Europe.

The rest of the first decade of the 21st Century would see some clubs (including United) purchased by overseas investors. Russians would be joined by Americans and the Chinese— the super-rich buying into English football was becoming C'est Chic! It was Chelsea who started the trend, and from a football viewpoint, the club was in a very healthy position when Abramovich had purchased them. They had already qualified for the Champions League just two months prior to the buyout by beating Liverpool 2–1 in the last game of the 2002–2003 season at Stamford Bridge.

Abramovich was a serious player and was looking at serious management to run the football side of his newly purchased club. Location-wise, Chelsea were a fashionable club and had started its ascent in the latter part of the 1990s to reach such heights on the pitch as well. Ruud Gullit, Gianfranco Zola, and Gianluca Vialli had all played for them, adding to the glamour. If Chelsea were going to comply with the force of nature that the Russian owner demanded that they would be with him at the helm, then they would need the very best manager around to help him achieve it. That wasn't going to be the present incumbent, Claudio Ranieri, in the eyes of Abramovich. Ranieri had taken the reigns at Chelsea in 2000 and had proved to be a very popular manager. Even though he hadn't brought them silverware, he had improved upon the tally of points that Chelsea accumulated in the league, and he had gotten them Champions League football for the coming season. Abramovich would need to tread carefully and get the fans on his side, so getting rid of Ranieri straight away was not an option for him. However, it became football's worst-kept secret that there would be a changing of the managerial guard at the Bridge as the 2003–2004 season progressed. Chelsea finished the season in second place to Arsenal's 'Invincibles' and even reached the semi-finals of the Champions League. It was the second time since the Premier League was introduced that United had not finished in either first or second place, the first being in the 2001–2002 season when Arsenal and Liverpool took those places, respectively.

Whilst Ranieri was aware that he was in an impossible position and simply could not win, he would be leaving Stamford Bridge with his head held high. Meanwhile, Roman Abramovich was busy looking for a new manager who could really take Chelsea to the next level. Chelsea had become the bright new thing in football, and they would need the bright new thing in football management to complement it. And the brightest of all stars was in Portugal, at Porto.

Enter José Mário dos Santos Mourinho Félix.

His Portuguese side were little fancied at the start of the 2003–2004 season as they entered the Champions League group stage. They had qualified out of Group F in second place to Real Madrid, and their reward was a tie against the winners of Group E—Manchester United. The first leg was played in Porto, and United got off to a good start when Quinton Fortune put the firm favourites into the lead. However, a brace from Benni

McCarthy, one in each half, was enough to give Porto a 2–1 win. United had Roy Keane sent off to make matters worse. Whilst it had been a bad day at the office for United, they had scored that important away goal, and the lead was a slender one for Porto. It was generally expected that United would finish off Porto in the second leg at Old Trafford two weeks later.

In the return leg, United took the lead on the 31st minute through a crisp header from Paul Scholes. The tie was level at 2–2 but United had the all-important away goal and would go through if no more goals were scored or indeed if they extended their lead. It looked like it would be the former that would see United progress as the game neared its end. Then, deep into stoppage time, Porto were awarded a free kick which was taken by Manchester United's nemesis in the first leg, Benni McCarthy. It wasn't the greatest of strikes from the South African international, but Tim Howard in the United goal, didn't deal with the routine kick and the ball found its way to Costinha, who put the ball into the net to send Porto through to the next round. Old Trafford was silenced. Whilst the Porto players celebrated, it was their manager's celebrations that caught the eye.

José Mourinho practically ran around Old Trafford like an Olympic runner. Mourinho flamboyantly celebrated the goal leaving his dugout, fists punching the air, as he sprinted down the touchline near to his celebrating players, and that dramatic celebration was probably the moment when Mourinho announced himself to the game—and certainly to Roman Abramovich.

He had taken the reigns at Porto in 2002 after a spell at Benfica and then-unknown club, União de Leiria, in his native Portugal. In his earlier years in coaching, he had been an interpreter for Sir Bobby Robson at both Sporting CP and Porto before becoming a coach under Sir Bobby at Barcelona, and later Louis van Gaal. Mourinho had gained valuable experience during that period, and it was only a matter of time before he went into management himself. It was at Porto that he would make his mark. Porto would go on to lift the Champions League trophy that season beating Monaco in the final 3–0.

Not surprisingly, the rest of the football world sat up and took notice, causing Roman Abramovich to make Mourinho his first managerial signing. That appointment catapulted Chelsea over the next couple of seasons as they won back-to-back titles in 2005 and 2006, and it meant that Manchester United didn't win the league for three seasons. Chelsea also went on to win the League Cup during this period and firmly cemented themselves as the Special Ones, just as Mourinho had self-proclaimed when he first stepped into Stamford Bridge. In that period, United had won just two trophies, beating Millwall 3–0 in the 2004 FA Cup final and Wigan 4–0 in a one-sided League Cup final in 2006. Blue had replaced red at the top table of English football.

Fans and pundits of the game were now asking if Manchester United's was over. If it was, then a lot of happy memories had been made and bragging rights earned, which could be dined out for a few years to come. But Sir Alex Ferguson didn't want to just have the memories, he wanted to make more. Reflection could wait!

He had been building awesome teams since 1990, which culminated in the successes of 1999. Now Chelsea had gotten in on the act and joined Arsenal in claiming to be the number one team in England. Both teams had put down significant markers. Sir Alex was building his next great team, and the return on investment would start to reap dividends in the latter part of the 2000s. But how did they get there?

Even though United had won three consecutive titles in 1999, 2000, and 2001, Sir Alex was very aware that in order to keep his side as competitive as he wanted them to be, he would have to keep progressing. The most pressing part of his job was knowing that, whilst he had greatness in his team, he would have to replace them with equal greatness or even better. His task was not impossible, though. This was Manchester United— the best club in the land, even if they weren't the best team. He would not have to do a hard sell for anyone to come and play for United, players would have to hard sell themselves. It was most definitely a buyer's market for Sir Alex. The new TV deal in 2001 had given rise to more fiscal gains for the top clubs, and Manchester United would have competition from other clubs who were prepared to spend big as well.

The first real issue that Sir Alex faced was in the goalkeeper department, and this was pretty evident in the 1999–2000 season when Mark Bosnich and Massimo Taibi had failed to live up to their billing. But how does anyone follow Peter Schmeichel? In the short term, he would rely on the trusty Raimond van der Gouw, but he was getting no younger. Replacing greatness with either the same or better proved to be an issue in the number one department, despite winning the league at a canter.

This was all to change in the 2000–2001 season when Fabien Barthez joined United from Monaco for £7.8 million The French international World Cup winner was an instant success and seemed to be the natural successor to Schmeichel. The move for Barthez was a signal for Bosnich to leave, and the Australian ended up at Stamford Bridge, an interesting move which didn't quite pay off for him. Teddy Sheringham may have been nearing his 35th birthday, but that didn't stop him from winning both the PFA (Professional Footballers' Association) and FWA (Football Writers' Award) Player of the Year awards as he was the leading scorer for United. Sir Alex knew that he would need a younger but just as prolific new striker, and he found this in Ruud van Nistelrooy. The signing of the young Dutch goal-machine was due to take place in the summer of 2000. However, doubts were raised about van Nistelrooy's fitness, and United wanted to carry out more medicals, which his club, PSV Eindhoven, refused. The deal was called off, and the next day, Manchester United would be vindicated when van Nistelrooy broke down in training, suffering a rupture to his anterior cruciate knee ligament.

United did eventually sign Ruud van Nistelrooy for £19 million the following year upon passing his medical. He was handed a 5-year contract. Everyone knew that it would be done and dusted after the aborted first attempt, and it prompted Teddy Sheringham to seek a move elsewhere. Teddy re-signed for Tottenham Hotspur at the end of the 2000–2001 season.

Ruud van Nistelrooy would see out his 5-year contract before moving to Real Madrid in 2006. During his time with United, he made 150 appearances and scored 95 goals—an amazing return. One of those goals was at Old Trafford against Arsenal on 24th October 2004, a penalty in a game that saw United win 2–0, ending Arsenal's 49-game unbeaten run. It was not the first time that he had taken a penalty against the Gunners. The previous season saw him miss a last-minute spot-kick in a game that finished goalless and was later dubbed the Battle of Old Trafford. Upon missing his spot kick, van Nistelrooy turned around and was immediately surrounded by Arsenal players, prompting a melee including several players from both sides. Tempers boiled over as Arsène Wenger and his players thought that van Nistelrooy had cheated and gotten Patrick Vieira sent off earlier in the game. The FA were clearly not happy with what had taken place at the end of the match, and as a result, Arsenal received a fine, as did five of their players, including Martin Keown.

Other significant signings in the summer of 2001 included the Argentinian midfielder Juan Sebastián Verón, Northern Ireland shot-stopper Roy Carroll, and French World Cup-winning defender Laurent Blanc.

Blanc had been outstanding for France in the 1998 World Cup but had missed the final as he had been controversially sent off in the semi-final victory over Croatia. One of the most endearing moments of that World Cup was of Blanc walking up to Fabien Barthez prior to kick-off and kissing his bald head. Now that both players had been re-united at club level, it would mean that the tradition could continue, especially in the Champions League games.

If the arrivals of 2001 had been significant, then one of the departures was very controversial. Jaap Stam's arrival in Manchester in 1998 proved to be a very successful one, and he was a key player in all the successes that came United's way over the next few seasons. He was a very important and imposing player at the heart of the United defence. In 2001, Stam was approaching his 30th birthday, and even though he had been sidelined by injury in the previous season, the Dutchman still had a lot to give. So, what prompted a parting of ways between the club and the player? It's a question that still prompts conversation today. One such theory is that Sir Alex had not been too happy when Stam had written his autobiography in 2001. In it, he detailed the dealings that took place between PSV Eindhoven and Manchester United when he signed in 1998 and claimed that the United manager had tapped him up. There were also suggestions that Stam was having an influence in the dressing room which his manager disapproved of.

Meanwhile, the Italian club, Lazio, had prepared a bid of £16.5 million for Stam, and after a poor game against Fulham, Sir Alex decided that the offer was too good for a player approaching 30, so the bid was accepted. Fans began asking: was it a personality clash or a financial decision? Either way, Jaap Stam would be leaving Old Trafford and effectively the last meeting between Stam and Ferguson took place on a petrol forecourt. It had turned into a sorry affair and was not befitting the way a great club and player should conclude their story together.

The real winners were Lazio. Any fears that Stam was past his sell-by date and that he had lost any pace were soon forgotten, and he stayed at the Italian club for three seasons before moving to AC Milan. He returned to his native Holland in 2006 to finish his career at Ajax. Overall, he played in a further 143 games after leaving United. In hindsight, it was felt by the fans that United had pulled the trigger too early, and having Stam around for a while longer would have been good for the new batch of Manchester United youngsters coming through, the likes of John O'Shea.

Sir Alex made admissions later that it was a mistake to sell Stam in 2001. Manchester United would win nothing the following season, and even though they were far from being a one-man team, perhaps they would have fared better with the Dutchman in the team.

Mistakes are easily remembered when it comes to Sir Alex Ferguson making them because they did not happen very often! And he certainly made amends for it some 12 months later when Rio Ferdinand made his way across the Pennines—United paid a then British record fee of £29.1 million from Leeds United in July 2002. Ferdinand had made a name for himself at West Ham United before a big-money move to Leeds took place in 2000, and he became an integral part of a team that reached the semi-finals of the Champions League. This made Sir Alex sit up and take notice of the 24-year-old central defender from Peckham.

Rio didn't get off to be the best start in his United career as he was blighted by injury. However, he returned at a pivotal part of the season when United hauled back an eight-point lead that Arsenal had to claim the league title and stop them from winning it consecutively. It was Manchester United's eighth Premier League victory in 11 seasons.

David Beckham had been with the club since he signed as a trainee at the age of 16. He made his first team debut at 17 and had just turned 18 when United claimed their first Premier League title in May 1993. A decade later, they had claimed their eighth. The 2002–2003 season had not been too kind for Beckham, though, as he endured an injury early on and was replaced by Ole Gunnar Solskjaer on the right-side of midfield. Beckham found it hard to get back into the team, and things turned for the worst after United were knocked out of the FA Cup by their arch-rivals, Arsenal. In the dressing room after the game, Sir Alex, in his fury from the cup exit, kicked a boot, which hit Beckham near the eye, causing a cut that required stitches. It was there for all the world to see, and speculation suggested that Beckham would be leaving United at the end of that season. Some suggested that it would be Ferguson who would be leaving after the incident.

However, it was Beckham who would do the leaving in the summer of 2003. Originally, it looked like his destination was going to be Barcelona, but in the end, it was Real Madrid who paid United £25 million for the services of the superstar. He had become a Galáctico, and the unveiling was very much in keeping with the theme and fanfare of becoming one. Real Madrid's president was Florentino Perez, and during the unveiling, he told the world's media, "He is a great player who is going to be part of the club's great history. He is a man of our times and a symbol of modern-day stardom, and what is certain is Real Madrid have signed Beckham because he's a great footballer and a very dedicated professional. His team spirit is unsurpassed, and he is one of the best English players of all time, and if only because of that, he is with us."

Soon after Beckham's departure, Dwight Yorke was also set to leave Manchester United when he signed for Blackburn Rovers for £2.6 million. Other notable departures were Laurent Blanc, who announced his retirement from the game; David May, who was given a free transfer; and Juan Sebastián Verón, who moved from the North-West of England for the West side of London when he signed for Chelsea for a fee of only £15 million.

The summer of 2003 also saw the departure of players that had played a major part in not only the treble-winning team of 1999 but the subsequent successes that followed. The need to replace like-for-like greatness (and more) was most needed in 2003. Incoming during the summer transfer window were the French forward, David Bellion, the Cameroonian midfielder Eric Djemba-Djemba, and the American goalkeeper Tim Howard. The Brazilian midfielder José Kléberson, who was a World Cup winner after Brazil had defeated Germany in the 2002 final in Japan, also put pen to paper and became a Red Devil.

The right side of midfield was an area that Sir Alex was particularly concerned. The departure of David Beckham had forced his hand, and whilst Ole Gunnar Solskjaer had performed admirably in the position, there was a void that needed filling.

Enter Cristiano Ronaldo!

Born in Madeira in Portugal, on 5th February 1985, Ronaldo had been with Sporting CP since the age of 12 and made his senior debut for them just four years later at the tender age of just 16. Tall, athletic, and an excellent dribbler with the ball at his feet, it would only be a matter of time before the bigger clubs in Europe came knocking on the door. Liverpool and Barcelona were touted as possible destinations for the rising star of world football during the 2002–2003 season, and Ronaldo had already met with Arsène Wenger in the November of that season. However, no firm bids were forthcoming, and Ronaldo continued to shine in Portugal during the season, making 25 first-team appearances and scoring three goals in the process.

In August 2003, Manchester United were invited to play Sporting CP at their new stadium. Ronaldo was on fire as the Portuguese team beat United 3–1. Not only could Sir Alex see the potential, but moreover, his players did as well and urged him to splash the cash and bring him to Manchester. United duly obliged and offered their Portuguese hosts £12.24 million after the game. The Portuguese club initially wanted Ronaldo to be loaned back to them to continue his development in his homeland. However, Sir Alex disagreed; he felt that the development of this exciting young and raw talent would be best served under his wing, and so he signed for Manchester

United on 12th August 2003. To show the faith that Sir Alex had with Ronaldo, he was offered the coveted number 7 shirt. This has been the number on the back of the shirt that George Best, Eric Cantona, and David Beckham had previously worn. It had become a numerical symbol of greatness at Old Trafford. And that was set to continue with the young man from Portugal— but not straight away. United knew that Ronaldo had the world at his feet and that his talent was so precious. It would have to be nurtured correctly—just like Sir Alex had done some 11 years earlier with the class of '92.

Ronaldo would play a total of 40 games in all competitions during his first season and put the ball into the net six times, the last of these was in the FA Cup final, where United comfortably beat Millwall 3–0. Manchester United finished third that season and did the same in the 2004–2005 season, before finishing runners-up to Chelsea in the next year. A consolation was that they won the League Cup that season, beating Wigan 4–0 in the final.

In his first three seasons in England, Ronaldo had played 137 games in all competitions and scored 27 goals. The nurturing process had been a successful one, even if Ronaldo had not yet experienced the glory of winning a Premier League title. He was 21, and the bad news for the rest of the league was that he had not yet reached his prime! Another astute signing came during the winter transfer window, when United secured the services of Louis Saha from Fulham for a fee of £12.4 million. Saha impressed with a goal on his debut against Southampton and would add another nine goals before the season ended.

Manchester United had broken their transfer record for a teenager when they signed Ronaldo and they did it again in 2004, but this time, it was someone much closer to home—33 miles from Manchester to be precise! Like Ronaldo, Wayne Rooney was born in 1985. He had been at Everton since the age of nine and made his senior debut for the Toffees in 2002. Rooney really announced his arrival later that season when the 16-year-old scored a wonder goal outside the box in the last minute of a league game against Arsenal at Goodison. His goal ended a 30-game unbeaten run for the North London club, and at the time, Rooney became the youngest player to score a Premier League goal.

Between 2002 and 2004, Rooney played for Everton 67 times in all competitions and bagged 15 goals. He was the hottest of properties and had even made his full England debut in 2003 before shining for his country in the 2004 European Championships that were held in Cristiano Ronaldo's home country, Portugal. Remarkably, Rooney scored four goals in the tournament, and he was still only 18. Everton were desperate to keep their protégé, and the Everton chairman, Bill Kenwright, offered Rooney a £50,000-a-week 5-year contract. Soon after, Newcastle United submitted a bid of £20 million that was quickly rejected by the Everton board. Rooney had shown the world what he could do, and if he was to move, it would have to be a club that could offer him the best chances of fulfilling his potential at the highest level. On 27th August, Wayne Rooney submitted a transfer request, United made a £20 million bid that was accepted, and Rooney became a Manchester United player. The bid from United included an additional £7 million in add-ons. United had got their man. Rooney was joined by Alan Smith, who signed from Leeds, and Gabriel Heinze, whom they purchased from PSG. They were also joined by youngsters Gerard Piqué and Giuseppe Rossi.

Although Newcastle United had not been successful with their bid for Wayne Rooney, they did manage to secure the services of one of the Class of '92 in the shape of Nicky Butt. Butt had been a marvellous servant to United but had found playing time harder to come by, and the move to St. James Park made sense for all concerned.

It would be another great servant of the club who had been part of those three games in May 1999 that would leave Old Trafford the following year, in 2005. The plaudits for Roy Keane during his tenure and captaincy at Old Trafford were long and worthy, but none more so than the game in Turin in April 1999. Keane played his last game for United on 18th September 2005. Keane was forced to come off the pitch with just minutes remaining, and it later transpired that it was a foot injury. Just a few weeks after the termination of his contract, Keane signed for his boyhood club, Celtic. It was the end of a magical era for United and Roy Keane.

Gary Neville was then given the Captain's armband. This

was a definite time of transition for Manchester United, and the tragic news of the death of United legend George Best made it a sombre time, not just for United but for the footballing world in general.

Whilst Gary was made skipper, Phil Neville had left the club and signed for Everton for an undisclosed fee. Brazilian midfielder José Kléberson signed for Turkish side Besiktas for £2.5 million.

United would make some shrewd signings with the capture of Edwin van der Sar from Fulham and the signing of Park Ji-Sung signed from PSV Eindhoven. Ben Foster also joined the United ranks and would offer cover for van der Sar.

The winter transfer business was also very shrewd with the signings of defenders Nemanja Vidic and Patrice Evra. Vidic signed from Spartak Moscow for £7 million, and Evra signed from Monaco for a reported fee of 5.5 million.

The summer signings as well as the winter ones had been significant, and with the building of buying and nurturing top young talent over the previous seasons, this would gel well for the oncoming 2006–2007 season. It had been three long years without a title success and had seen United not even qualify out of the Group Stages of the UEFA Champions League during that period—the first time that it had happened since the 1994–1995 season.

Now was the time to reclaim it. The final business in terms of comings and goings in the summer of 2006 would see them do exactly that. There was only one player that was forthcoming during the summer, and that was Michael Carrick. A central midfielder whose passing skills had been exquisite in that department. Originally from the North-East of England, Carrick had most noticeably served both West Ham, and later, Tottenham. Manchester United had approached Spurs early in the summer but had their bid rejected. Sir Alex was very close to having the team that he wanted and saw Carrick as the final piece of the jigsaw as the replacement for Roy Keane. On 28th July, Tottenham announced that a deal had been agreed, with a fee reported to be in the region of £18.6 million. Carrick was given the Number 16 shirt previously worn by Roy Keane.

Making their way out of Old Trafford was Ruud van

Nistelrooy, who moved to Real Madrid, followed by David Bellion, Sylvan Ebanks-Blake, Paul McShane, Luke Steele, and Liam Miller.

The January transfer window saw United acquire the services of Henrik Larrson and Polish goalkeeper Tomasz Kuszczak on loan, and making way were Tim Howard and David Jones.

Manchester United started the league campaign on fire and won each of the first four games. The opening day of the season had seen them host Fulham at Old Trafford, and United had raced into a four-goal lead before the 20-minute mark, and the game ended 5–1. Charlton Athletic, Watford, and Tottenham were then duly defeated. The first loss of the season came courtesy of Arsenal, who came away from Old Trafford with a 1–0 victory. United followed this up with a 1–1 draw at newly promoted Reading, and this result knocked United off of the top spot. Had the bubble burst after the first four games? The answer was an emphatic no, as United picked up a maximum 18 points from their next six games. In fact, the only time they were not in pole position all season was after that game at Reading. They reclaimed it after beating Newcastle in the next game by 2–0, and they never lost it again. United finished the campaign as champions, winning a possible 28 out of 38 games, finishing six points clear of their nearest rivals Chelsea and with 21 more than third-placed Liverpool.

Manchester United also reached the final of the FA Cup, and it would be Chelsea who would exact revenge for beating them in the title race with a drab 1–0 victory. Didier Drogba netting the winner in the 116th minute in extra-time. It was the first final back at the newly rebuilt Wembley. The defence of the League Cup was short-lived too, as United were beaten at Roots Hall, the home of Southend United, by a solitary goal in the fourth round. Not surprisingly, that was the biggest cup upset that season.

United would also have a very good campaign in the Champions League. In fact, it was a very good year for other English clubs in general. Three teams qualified for the semi-finals. United would face AC Milan, and the other semi-final would see Liverpool playing Chelsea. However, it was not an all-English final, as United lost to the Italian giants 5–3 on aggregate. Liverpool beat Chelsea on penalties to progress to the final, where they faced AC Milan for the second time in as many years. AC Milan won the final by 2–1, and the English clubs would rue the fact that they had three teams in the semis, but not one of them lifted the trophy. Would there be another chance for English clubs to play each other in the final again? The answer was not far away at all.

Manchester United had dominated the league once more and were back where they belonged. This was evident in the PFA Team of the Year, where no less than eight players made the 11, and Cristiano Ronaldo picked up a staggering eight individual awards for his performances over the season. Sir Alex Ferguson won the Premier League's Manager of the Season award too.

If the 2006–2007 season had not been remarkable enough already, it was also the 50th anniversary of the Busby Babes' first matches in Europe. The event was marked by a charity football match which had been organised by UEFA to commemorate 50 years since the signing of the Treaty of Rome. The match was played against a team of the best players from Europe's top clubs at the time.

The 2006–2007 campaign had heralded the comeback of Manchester United and the following season saw them fully cement their place at the top—and them some!

To continue the progress, United made three significant signings during the summer of 2007. Owen Hargreaves was brought in from Bayern Munich on 1st July 2007. The following day, Nani and Anderson arrived for a combined fee of £30 million, both from Portuguese teams. Nani from Sporting CP and the Brazilian Anderson from Porto. On the same day, United made Tomasz Kuszczak a permanent signing. Perhaps the strangest of all transfers occurred in that summer as well, and it turned into a right saga, the likes never seen before. Carlos Tevez had played for West Ham United the previous season, and it was reported that the Argentinian striker had agreed a deal to join Manchester United. This was blocked by West Ham, as he was under contract to the East London club in 2010. However, Tevez was owned by a third party and represented by his agent, Kia Joorabchian. West Ham would not sell unless they received the majority of the transfer fee. Both West Ham and United sought FIFA's assistance to rule on the third-party ownership, and FIFA recommended that the case be submitted to the Court of Arbitration for Sport. At that stage, Joorabchian got involved and issued a writ "to compel West Ham to release the registration of Carlos Tevez in accordance with the contracts entered into between both parties." This unprecedented situation in the UK was settled with the third-party paying West Ham £2 million to release his contract, and the case didn't ever go to court. United had got their man once again. Third-party ownership of players was rightly banned in 2015.

It was the summer that saw the retirement of Ole Gunnar Solskjaer. He had been a great servant to United and had always given his all, either from the bench or a starting berth, and of course, he will always be remembered for scoring the final goal in United's treble-winning campaign. Other players to leave were Kieran Richardson, who signed for Sunderland; Giuseppe Rossi who joined Villarreal; and Alan Smith, who departed for Newcastle United. The final outgoing transfer was Gabriel Heinze, who signed for Real Madrid.

The domestic cups campaign in the 2007–2008 season was a disappointing one for United. In the FA Cup as United went out to eventual winners, Portsmouth, at the quarter-final stage. In the League Cup, their exit came at Coventry City in just the third-round stage of the competition.

It would be the League and Champions League which would bring United glory.

It wasn't to be the greatest start, though, as they went about defending the league title. Two consecutive draws at home to Reading and away at Portsmouth, followed by a 1–0 defeat at Manchester City, saw United sitting in 17th place. It was a rude awakening for the club, and then Manchester United became, well, Manchester United, winning the next eight league games and reclaiming the top spot. It then became a tussle between Chelsea and United on who would be in top place over the coming months. Manchester United claimed the top spot, on 15th March 2008, when a Ronaldo goal in the 76th minute was enough to give them a 1–0 victory at Derby County. After that game, they didn't lose the top spot again all season, although it would go down to the last match of the season before United could claim consecutive titles. A 2–0 away win at Wigan courtesy of a Ronaldo penalty in the 33rd minute and a goal by the evergreen Ryan Giggs was enough to make it back-to-back title victories. The margin of victory had been six points over Chelsea the season before, and now it was down to two. United had lived on their nerves and saw it through. Exactly 10 days after the final game of the Premier League season, there would be another tussle with Chelsea. This time it would be in the Champions League final, an all-English final for the very first time in the competition.

All roads led to Moscow for both teams after a gruelling campaign.

Chelsea had finished top of Group B, and United had done the same in Group F. Chelsea had played Schalke 04, Rosenborg, and Valencia on the way to topping the group, and United had played Roma, Sporting CP, and Dynamo Kiev in theirs.

Chelsea's route to the final in the knockout stages saw them defeat Olympiacos of Greece 3–0 on aggregate, and then the Turkish Club, Fenerbahçe, by 3–2 over two legs in the quarter-final. For the second year running, they would face Liverpool in the semi-final, and again, this would guarantee a final berth for at least one English club. This time, it would be the Blues of Chelsea that would make the final with a 4–3 win over the two legs.

United met Lyon in the Round of 16 and went through 2–1 on aggregate. They were then paired with Roma, winning both legs to seal a 3–0 victory. Manchester United had made it through to the semi-final and standing in their way was Barcelona. There was no semi-final heartbreak like they'd had the previous season, and United went through 1–0 on aggregate.

A crowd of 67,310 people packed into the Luzhniki Stadium, in Moscow. on 21st May 2008, to witness the first all-English final in history, with millions around the world watching on the TV or the big screens.

United's team:
van der Sar, Brown, Ferdinand, Vidic, Evra, Hargreaves, Carrick, Scholes, Ronaldo, Rooney, Tevez. Substitutes: Giggs, Nani, Anderson, Kuszczak, O'Shea, Fletcher, Silvestre.

Chelsea's team:
Cech, Essien, Carvalho, Terry, Cole (A), Ballack, Makélélé, Lampard, Cole (J), Drogba, Malouda. Substitutes: Cudicini, Shevchenko, Obi, Kalou, Alex, Belletti, Anelka.

Ronaldo gave United the lead on 26 minutes, climbing to meet the ball in the air and powerfully heading it into the net. Lampard levelled for Chelsea on the stroke of half-time. There would be no further goals in the second half, nor in extra-time. The game would be decided by penalties.

Tevez, Carrick, Hargreaves, and Nani had all successfully converted theirs for the team in red. However, Ronaldo missed the third penalty. Chelsea had converted their first four courtesy of Ballack, Belletti, Lampard, and Ashley Cole. Then John Terry stepped up to take the fifth one. If he scored, Chelsea would be crowned champions of Europe. The stadium went quiet. John Terry's run-up was not a good one, and he slipped as he struck the ball. The post was rattled. The United net had not been. Manchester United had their reprieve, and the penalty shoot-out moved into sudden death. Anderson and Kalou were calm heads as they both converted for their respective clubs to make it 5–5. Up next was Ryan Giggs. Again, he kept a cool head as was befitting for a player of his calibre and standing, and he made it 6–5. Anelka stepped up, but van der Sar made the save, and utter elation for United followed as they had won the Champions League for the second time in nine years and the third in their history.

Sir Alex Ferguson had done it once more. He had built his third great team and, prior to the final, had perhaps given his greatest pre-match talk. Many years later, Patrice Evra told *The Players Tribune* what he told the players. "We were in the dressing room when the boss came in. As usual, the music stopped. You could hear a pin drop. Then, Ferguson said, 'I've already won.' We looked at each other. He said, 'I've already won. We don't even need to play this game'. We were like, 'What is he talking about? The game hasn't even started.' Then Ferguson turned to me, 'Look at Patrice,' he said. 'He's got 24 brothers and sisters. Imagine what his mother had to do to put food on the table.' Then he turned to Wayne Rooney. 'Look at Wayne. He grew up in one of the toughest parts of Liverpool.' Then he turned to Park Ji-Sung: 'Look at Ji, he's come all the way from South Korea.' As the boss talked about our stories, we began to realise that he was referring to a fellowship. We were not just a football team, we were people from every corner of the world, from all kinds of cultures, races, and religions. And now we were there, together in a dressing room in Moscow, fighting for a common cause. Through football, we had become brothers. 'THIS is my victory!' Ferguson said."

Patrice Evra continued, "We all got goosebumps. Then we went out and won the Champions League."

This was Manchester United in May 2008.

EPILOGUE
10 Years After 1999

Substance.

***

ON 17ᵀᴴ JANUARY 2009, Manchester United went top of the league for the first time in the 2008–2009 season. They had just beaten Bolton Wanderers at the Reebok Stadium by 1–0. It had taken until the 90ᵗʰ minute for United to take the lead, and the goal-scorer was Dimitar Berbatov, who met a cross from Carlos Tevez to head the ball into the Bolton net.

This was a position that they would keep for the remainder of the campaign as they went on to win their third league title in a row. It was the second time they had achieved this feat—no team had done this twice before. They finished the season on 90 points, four more than their nearest rivals, Liverpool. United strongly competed on four fronts and got to at least the semi-finals of each cup competition they entered.

The champions of Europe also became champions of The World. Unlike their last controversial foray in the FIFA Club World Cup in 2000, United did not have to play in the group stages and came into it at the semi-final stage, as did LDU Quito from Ecuador, the CONMEBOL Club Champions. Both teams would reach the final. United had defeated the Japanese side, Gamba Osaka, in a thrilling match 5–3 in their semi-final; Gamba Osaka had qualified by beating the Mexican side Pachuca 2–0.

The final was played at the International Stadium in Yokohama, Japan, on 21ˢᵗ December 2008, in front of a crowd of

68,682. The only goal came in the 73rd minute and was converted by Wayne Rooney. There would be no repeat of United not participating in the FA Cup, and no pressure from the FA or the Government this time.

They would also add the League Cup to the trophy cabinet as well, after overcoming Tottenham Hotspur 4–1 on penalties. Ben Foster was the hero in goal on that occasion.

The FA Cup was the only competition in which they didn't reach the final. This time they would be on the receiving end of a penalty shoot-out defeat following a goalless draw against Everton.

The Champions of Europe would defend their title with stealth as they reached the final for the second consecutive time, their third in 10 seasons. United finished top of Group E with two wins and four draws, securing 10 points, as they pitted their wits against Villareal from Spain, Aalborg BK from Denmark, and Scottish champions Celtic. Rod Stewart released a song in 1977 called 'You're In My Heart' in which the former gravedigger referenced Celtic and United in the song as he supported both of them. Not surprisingly, Stewart was spotted in the crowd at both legs. He couldn't really lose, but one suspects that he would have been happy if both games had finished all square instead of just one of them! A Berbatov brace and a goal from Wayne Rooney had been enough to give United a 3–0 win their home leg, before drawing the game at Celtic Park 1–1, with Ryan Giggs netting in the 84th minute. His goal had cancelled out Celtic's opener in the 13th minute, scored by Scott McDonald.

The route to the final was a stern one for the holders. Firstly, Inter Milan were beaten 2–0 on aggregate. United then were able to exact revenge against Porto in the quarter-finals to set up yet another all-English semi-final, guaranteeing the fifth consecutive final with a team from the Premier League in the final. Arsenal had reached the final in 2006, where they lost to Barcelona, so they were hoping to go one better and meet them in the final again, but Manchester United stood in their way and proved too much for the Gunners, winning the tie 4–1 on aggregate. After taking a slender 1–0 lead at Old Trafford, United turned on the style at the Emirates, winning 3–1. John O'Shea had been the unlikely scorer for United in the first leg against Arsenal, with the goals away scored by Park and two from Ronaldo.

And so, it was Manchester United who were to play Barcelona in the 2009 final, and if they were to win the game, it would be the first time that a British club would successfully defend the Champions League. It had been done before in the old format when it was called the European Cup, with both Liverpool and Nottingham Forest, but not since the new format had been introduced in 1993.

However, it wasn't to be as Barcelona won the game 2–0. The BBC reported after the game: "Manchester United's attempt to make history and become the first club to defend the Champions League ended in failure against Barcelona in Rome's Stadio Olimpico. Manager Sir Alex Ferguson's hopes of repeating last year's triumph against Chelsea barely got off the ground, as they ended up being well beaten by a Barcelona side inspired by the genius of Argentine superstar Lionel Messi. United started the final, played in stifling heat, as if retaining their crown would be little more than a formality, creating a host of early chances against the nervous-looking Catalans, with Cristiano Ronaldo a constant threat. But once Samuel Eto'o scored at Edwin van der Sar's near post in the 10th minute after escaping Nemanja Vidic, the credits were rolling on their bid to add the Champions League to the Premier League for the second successive season.

Barcelona's peerless midfield pair of Andres Iniesta and Xavi ruled midfield with a display of passing perfection, starving United of further opportunities to strike at a defence weakened by injuries and suspension. Xavi hit the post with a free-kick, and Thierry Henry was denied by van der Sar before Messi crowned a glorious personal performance with a stunning header to clinch victory with 20 minutes remaining. He made a mockery of his tiny stature to rise and head home Xavi's cross— and in that magical moment, any hopes United harboured of a recovery were snuffed out.

If the showdown between Messi and Ronaldo was billed as the spectacular sub-plot within this showpiece, there was only one winner as Barcelona's playmaker terrorised United throughout. Ronaldo, for all his obvious frustrations that ended almost inevitably in a yellow card for a late barge on Carles

Puyol, never stopped running, but this was not to be his night or United's."

"Ferguson warned in the build-up that Iniesta—arguably the game's most influential performer—and Xavi could put opponents 'on a carousel' with their passing, and his prediction proved ominously correct as United were on a rough ride after the optimism of those opening 10 minutes. Once Barcelona had settled after the early goal, there was no way back for United as several changes in formation failed to produce a spark and Wayne Rooney was unable to exert any influence on events, first from the left flank and then from the centre. And as Barcelona's name was carved on the giant trophy at the final whistle, with the celebrations of the Catalan fans a sharp contrast to the subdued Manchester United supporters, there was no doubting their right to claim Europe's elite trophy for the third time. Ryan Giggs took the place of the suspended Darren Fletcher in the United line-up—and for the first 10 minutes, they penned a nervous Barcelona back in their own territory. The game was only two minutes old when Barcelona keeper Victor Valdes fumbled Ronaldo's free-kick, and only the crucial intervention of former United defender Gerard Pique, prevented Ji-Sung Park turning in the rebound. Ronaldo was then twice narrowly off target before Barcelona made their first serious incursion into United territory. And it was to devastating effect as they turned the opening exchanges upside down to take the lead."

"Barcelona will credit the brilliance of Eto'o, but it was a cheap shot from United's viewpoint, as the Cameroon striker was allowed to escape by Vidic and keeper van der Sar's effort to block the effort at his near post was flimsy, to put it kindly. It was against the run of play but gave Barcelona a visible injection of confidence and adrenalin, allowing Messi to pull the strings up front and Xavi and Iniesta to take control of midfield. Iniesta may have been an injury doubt prior to this final, but there was little evidence of fitness problems as he produced a virtuoso demonstration of the modern midfield arts, leaving United to chase in vain in an attempt to regain possession for the latter stages of the opening half. In one magical moment, all three of Vidic, Michael Carrick, and Rooney were foiled in an attempt to take the ball away from Messi, with the Argentine eventually forcing a foul. Rooney was a peripheral figure, pushed to the margins of the game on the left flank. He was too important a figure to be starved of possession and influence in this system, and it was no surprise when Ferguson pushed him inside as half-time approached."

"Ferguson made another switch during the interval, sending on Carlos Tevez for the ineffective Anderson, a positive move that reflected United's failure to build on their early domination. It was not a quick fix as Barcelona simply continued in their imperious stride after the break, Thierry Henry tricking his way inside Rio Ferdinand, only to be denied by the legs of van der Sar. Xavi then almost doubled Barcelona's lead with a 20-yard free-kick following Vidic's foul on Messi. He beat van der Sar with his curling effort, but it rebounded off an upright to safety."

"United were struggling to get a clear sight of Barcelona's goal, and in a bid to remedy this problem, Ferguson sent on Dimitar Berbatov for Park with 25 minutes remaining. The change had no chance to take effect before Barcelona deservedly went two-up five minutes later. Xavi was the creator with a cross that looked too high for Messi, but he expertly soared to send a header over van der Sar. United looked to mount an instant response, with Valdes blocking crucially from Ronaldo, but there was no way back, and it was Barcelona who looked more likely to add to their lead. van der Sar saved well from Puyol as Barcelona dominated until the final whistle—and not even the most partisan Manchester United follower can doubt that Pep Guardiola deserved to round off a dream first season in charge by adding the Champions League to the La Liga title and the Spanish Cup."

The BBC report continued: "Barcelona had joined Manchester United in the ranks of winning the Continental Treble."

The biggest incoming transfer before the start of the campaign had been Dimitar Berbatov, who had been a deadline day signing from Tottenham Hotspur for a fee of £30.75 million. Twins, Fabio and Rafael were both signed from Brazilian team Fluminense for an undisclosed fee. And in the January transfer window, United bought in Ritchie De Laet from Stoke City and Zoran Tošic from Partizan Belgrade, both fees were undisclosed.

Four players left, and they were Chris Eagles to Burnley, Mikael Silvestre to Arsenal, Louis Saha went to Everton, whilst Dong Fangzhuo left the club.

At the start of the 2008–2009 season, United had a player called Lee Martin on the books. He was soon loaned out to Nottingham Forest. 20 years earlier, at the start of the 1988–1989 Season, United had another player called Lee Martin on their books. That one didn't go to Nottingham Forest on loan, but he would be in the team that defeated them in the third round of the FA Cup in 1990 at the City Ground. He would also go on to score the winning goal in *that* 1990 FA Cup Final replay, the one that gave Alex Ferguson his first trophy and the one that ensured the end of the Scotsman's time on football's death row.

The name of these two United players, 20 years apart, may well be serendipitous, but serve to be a nexus between the events that took United away from its fall into its rise and how Alex Ferguson was able to build his first great team—one that would satisfy his thirst to becoming THE team to beat, not just in the cup competitions.

The achievements of the second and third great empires are well documented in this and previous chapters of this book. During the latter part of the 1960s all the way through to the early 1990s, Manchester United had been cup collectors ever since winning the old First Division trophy in 1967, although it would be remiss not to mention that they had won the Second Division trophy in the 1974–1975 season. Between 1968 and 1993, eight teams would lay claim to be champions of England, and Manchester United would not feature in this list over this 26-year period. Some have called this period the barren years, yet during this time the club still won:

The European Cup in 1967–1968
Final v Benfica 4–1 (a.e.t.)

The FA Cup in 1976–1977
Final v Liverpool 2–1

The FA Cup in 1982–1983
Final v Brighton & Hove Albion 2–2
Final Replay v Brighton & Hove Albion 4–0

The FA Cup in 1984–1985
Final v Everton (H) 1–0 (a.e.t.)

The FA Cup in 1989–1990
Final v Crystal Palace 3–3
Final Replay v Crystal Palace 1–0

The European Cup Winners Cup in 1990–1991
Final v Barcelona 2–1

The League Cup in 1991–1992
Final v Nottingham Forest 1–0

The haul of seven major trophies during this period reminds us that Manchester United were still a very relevant and active team, but after the title winning season in 1966–1967, no one at the club could have possibly foreseen not claiming this for such a long period of time after.

It would be hard pressed for anyone (including Liverpool supporters) not to concede that Ferguson built three great teams in this 20-year period, from 1989 until 2009. And the building process was different on occasion in terms of its methodology, and it was fitting of its times. In his 2012 autobiography, *Red,* Gary Neville breaks this down. "What made the 2008 triumphs so special was how the boss moved with the times. If the 1994 team was obviously British and muscular, and the 1999 vintage a little more refined, and by 2008 we'd taken on a continental feel. We might still play 4–4–2 at times, but there was no comparison with a decade earlier. We had so much variation. Sometimes our opponents wouldn't know who was centre-forward. Accused in the past of fielding a naive, gung-ho team, the manager had embraced new ideas."

Being able to move with the times was Sir Alex's greatest asset. Closely followed by his burning passion as the guardian of the club in so many ways. He could do this specifically and generically with the same vigour and end result. Eric Cantona in 1995 at Selhurst Park, and the subsequent fall out and ban is perhaps the finest specific example during his tenure. The way that the mercurial Frenchman came back was testament to the skills of his manager.

A strong case for his generic skills would centre around one of his own players, but not so much on the domestic front, but moreover, the international stage. On 23rd September 2003, Rio Ferdinand had failed to take a drug test at the Carrington training ground after being one of the four players to be picked out of a hat by the UK Sport drugs testing team, who had arrived that morning unannounced. Each player was told that they could shower and then have the test. After taking his shower, Ferdinand left the training ground and was later spotted out shopping. In the meantime, the club tried to get their central defender back so that the test could be carried out. By the time they had reached him, the testing team had left the complex.

However, Ferdinand took the test the day after. His failure not to take the test as planned was deemed to be sufficient to press misconduct charges against the player, and the hearing was set for the start of 2004. In the meantime, England were playing crucial European Championship qualifiers for the tournament in Portugal in the summer of 2004. The FA had decided that it would be better for the image of the game for Rio Ferdinand not to be picked for those games, and pressure was put on the England Manager, Sven-Göran Eriksson, not to pick him. This led to days of tabloid speculation of 'will he or won't he pick Ferdinand.' Inevitably, this would lead to Ferdinand's omission. Not only would the decision be the headline news on the back pages but would also reach the front pages as the decision taken angered his international teammates, who strongly felt that Ferdinand had been hung out to dry by the FA. The reasons as to why this reached the front pages was that the players were so incensed by the decision that they threatened to go on strike in solidarity. A most noticeable voice of dissent came from Gary Neville, who was dubbed "the most hated footballer in the country" at the time. With all 23 players voting to go on strike and it looked very much like this would be the end result. The FA feared that as a result of the impossible situation, England would have been omitted from the finals without playing.

It was now or never. Fergie had decided that even though this was an England issue, he would have to step in, and make his case that a decision for the likes of Gary Neville to leave the squad could impact and undermine Manchester United, as much as it would do for England. Ferguson sympathised with Neville's cause, but the players had made their point and taken it as far as they could. For the sake of football in general, the strike could not take place, and therefore, the games would go ahead. The intervention made by the Manchester United manager may not have been the only factor, but it was a key one none-the-less.

Sir Alex Ferguson was not just the manager of Manchester United Football Club, he was its custodian. He was a father figure to his players. He was a project manager. He had the right stakeholders to ensure that the vision went from the drawing board to the pitch, from the cleaners to the boardroom. Everyone had a part to play, and everyone rose to the challenge. They were all important cogs in the wheel, that was the United way. He was the architect of excellence that came back to Old Trafford and re-invented itself—not once, not twice, but THREE times.

None of this would have been in the job description back in 1986, but this is exactly what happened.

If Sir Alex Ferguson had been put in charge of Manchester United's welfare in 2016, as opposed to the 30 years before, there would have been no way that he would have been afforded the time to build his three great dynasties—or would he have been? Martin Edwards and the board deserve a lot of credit for seeing his vision and recognising his hard work, and not giving into popular opinions in the late 1980s and very early 1990s.

Football's dictatorships simply don't allow this in the 21st Century. Take Leicester City, for example. They defied the odds of 5000/1 to win the Premier League in 2016. They were crowned champions in May 2016, and on 23rd February 2017, Claudio Ranieri was relieved of his managerial duties, not even a year after from achieving success, he was sacked.

Another example is Tottenham Hotspur, who reached the final of the Champions League in May 2019 for the first time in their history, before losing to Liverpool 2–0. Mauricio Pochettino did not even see the whole of 2019 out before he was sacked.

There are plenty of other examples.

So, what chance would Sir Alex have had with two consecutive finishes outside the top 10, despite winning the FA Cup in the second season? Managers are sacked even if they have just won their last game—such is modern football!

Football bosses are trigger happy in the 21st Century. It's all about now and today—tomorrow is a luxury that football does not lend itself to, anymore. Social media has also played a major part, and it's not always a positive one. The fan is generally fickler these days, and a lot of this does stem from having owners that demand instant success without building a foundation at times. It trickles down from the boardroom to the terraces very quickly, and now everyone has that voice, and it's instant. Your team loses, and social media feeds are full of doom and gloom, and the inevitable locking horns from the glass half-empty and glass half-full brigades commence in true keyboard-warrior combat. Even if your team wins, then the naysayers will still voice their concerns, whether they have made a salient point or not! It's revolution, not evolution.

Sir Alex Ferguson's Manchester United's journey is one of heritable value. One of nurture, and change, when it was necessary, whilst never taking his eyes off the prize. This was true of Arsène Wenger's tenure at Arsenal as well. It can be no coincidence that both of these legendary managers stayed at the helm for as long as they did, without proper succession planning, and won as much as they did as they extended their trophy cabinets. It's just that Sir Alex Ferguson achieved his for longer periods and added more silverware. And he did it with more style.

And, of course, he gave us those three games in May.

ACKNOWLEDGEMENTS

***

THERE ARE A NUMBER of people and organisations that a writer is very grateful to when researching material for a sports book that has been floating around in their senses for a number of years.

Due diligence is a necessity, and sometimes can be the worst part of putting together a book such as this one. Putting pen to paper (or rather, fingers on the keyboard) is the easiest part, especially when you get into the zone and just type away. I can honestly say, with hand on heart, that the research element took me to some fascinating places with people I could have talked to for a lot longer than was anticipated.

It must have been the most captivating period of time to support, play for, work for, or write about Manchester United between the years of 1998 and 1999. The fans that I spoke to were simply magnificent, and just asking them to talk about individual games, or the season as a whole, took them back to a period in their lives that may also have been tainted with sadness, over the passing of loved ones, for example. Some of these people were not overly religious types, but it was the 'Church of Manchester United' that had kept them going.

I asked a simple question, which may have taken just a few words if I had written it down, but what I got back in return was waxing lyrical at its finest. I smiled to myself when those fans told their stories, even with their facial expressions. They do say that every picture tells a story, and I saw that either face-to-face, in person, or on Zoom calls. Even the sentences that I received back via e-mail meant that I could sense the passion, the glory, and the trials and tribulations in their words—the funny stories and the sad ones as well.

There are some really good United groups on social media whom I reached out to as well. One in particular that can be found on Facebook is called 'From the banks of the River Irwell.' At the time of writing (December 2022), it had around 7,000 followers, and quite frankly, it deserves a lot more. I would break down a particular chapter and ask them for their feedback and memories of the game in question, and I received some really great pointers and stories in no time at all. I found the group very supportive of where I was going with this project, and that spurred me on to continue.

I don't doubt that for a second that Manchester United fans were put through the mixer during the 1998–1999 season and came out of it in a world of unending triumph. The thing was that I really kind of expected this from the fans, but perhaps I didn't realise just how much. However, what I really didn't expect was to feel as much passion from the journalists I spoke to. It was totally wonderful to speak at length to Neil Custis, for instance. Neil is now *The Sun's* football correspondent, covering United as he has since 1999. His knowledge is breath-taking, and so is his enthusiasm for the job he does.

And he doesn't even support Manchester United!

Another journalist I spoke to at length is Stuart Mathieson, who retired as Neil Custis' equivalent for *The Manchester Evening News* in 2016. I had read an article about him when he retired that said he was a 'laptop for hire,' so I was very excited to see how he could help me when I made my first introduction to him. Imagine my disappointment upon finding out that he had even retired from being a 'laptop for hire.' I shouldn't have worried, though. He was always helpful on calls and responded to my (many) texts and e-mails very quickly when I needed his reports, memoirs, and thoughts on a particular topic that I wanted to cover.

John Wragg was also extremely helpful to me, and I was particularly enamoured with a lovely story when this fine freelance journalist emailed me back in March 2022. He was working for *The Daily Express* in 1999 when United played Arsenal in THAT FA Cup semi-final replay win at Villa Park.

He interviewed Sir Bobby Charlton in the car park after the win, and I just had to include that story in this book.

Susan and Clive Tyldesley were both very helpful and gave me permission to use what I needed from Clive's autobiography, *Not For Me, Clive.* I love Clive's passion with his microphone and his laptop.

Steve Bruce deserves credit for writing the foreword for the book. Huge thanks to West Bromwich Albion too, who Steve was managing at the time. I could have received emails back from West Brom telling me not to bother their manager, but I didn't. They were very helpful. Class club.

Many thanks to all those fine scribes, players, and fans of the beautiful game—top people as well.

I have read some fantastic books about this marvellous period, but it still amazed me when I started to look at how many books had been written about Manchester United. My last count was well over 500, and I am still pretty sure that I have not encountered all of them! I guess this is what happens when you have the worldwide support of this famous club. One day I am going to compare United's tally of books to those of Liverpool and the likes of Real Madrid and Barcelona to get a really good comparison. I am indebted to ALL those writers that came before me, whether it be fiction or non-fiction. I am pretty sure there will be a lot more to come after me as well; such is the draw of the Red Devils. They will always be relevant and worth writing about.

I took the idea for this book to my late father back in November 2021. Despite suffering with ill health, he told me to write it because he could see my passion for this wonderful sporting story, and his encouragement to me was first class—as he was as a human being. Sadly, he passed away from prostate cancer in March 2022. It is so fitting that Prostrate Cancer UK have got involved with us and supported this book, and some of the proceeds are going to this great charity organisation.

The encouragement my father gave me has continued with my stepmother, Hilary, and my brother and sister, Darren and Suzanne.

To my brilliant nephews, George and Jake, and nieces, Abi and Jodie.

Thanks to my wonderful partner, Claire, and the boy we call 'Albert Dock', even though his name is Alex! I must have driven them mad with my heavy typing style, but they have been so supportive and have provided some great suggestions, just like Pat (Claire's mum) did. As was the rest of my family and friends.

The same can be said for my agent, Simon Goodyear, who is also an author of around a dozen books and counting. Thanks for taking my call when you did, and thanks for all your help and support on this project. Thanks also to David Shuttle for critiquing the manuscript and providing useful feedback.

A special mention has to go to everyone at Morgan Lawrence, my publishers. Mathew Mann, Barrie Pierpoint, Lee Clark, Amy Memory, Harry Worgan, and Peter Taylor.

Now a big thanks to some amazing women in my life:

My Mother, who passed away in 2003 (another United championship year)—Barb, I love you X.

To my Nan, Dolly, who also left us this year. Nearly 100 years on this planet, and absolutely beautiful in all of them.

And finally, to the two most important people in my life, my daughters. I am so proud to be your dad. Bethany May Carless and Emily Grace Carless—I am in awe of you and love you so very much. Keep on being brilliant X.

And finally, a BIG thank you to YOU for reading this book. I hope you enjoy every page of it.

It's been a pleasure.

Rob Carless

BIBLIOGRAPHY

***

Managing My Life: My Autobiography—Alex Ferguson

Dwight Yorke: The Official Biography—Hunter Davies

The Impossible Treble—Steve Bartram, Paul Davies and Ben Hibbs

My Side—David Beckham

Red —Gary Neville

Manchester United Official Yearbook 1999—Cliff Butler with Ivan Ponting

Not For Me, Clive: Stories from the Voice of Football —Clive Tyldesley

Factory Fairy-Tales—Ged Duffy

Andy Cole: The Autobiography—Andy Cole

Fast Forward: The Autobiography—Andy Cole

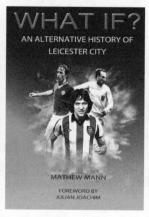

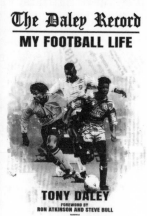

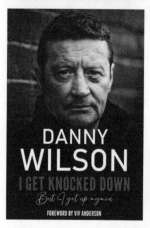
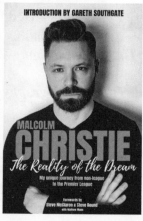
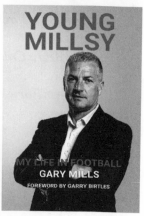